PENGUIN BUSINESS

CATALYST

The late Chandramouli Venkatesan, author of *Get Better at Getting Better* and *Transform*, was a corporate veteran with over twenty-six years of experience in the industry. He worked with Asian Paints, Cadbury/Mondelez, Mirc Electronics/Onida and Pidilite. He served in various senior capacities, including as CEO and managing director. While the bulk of his work life had been in business and P&L leadership roles, there was a three-year period when he did a cross-functional stint as the HR head for Cadbury India, which further developed his understanding of what makes people successful.

Chandramouli was a keen golfer, a sports enthusiast and believed in holding his life in balance. This, coupled with his sense of values and spirituality, led him to believe that every person must impact society positively. He conducted numerous speaking sessions, which have benefited over 1000 people, and mentored and guided many others to be successful in their careers. He passed away in 2020 at the age of fifty-four.

catalyst

The ultimate strategies on
how to win at work and in life

CHANDRAMOULI VENKATESAN

PENGUIN
BUSINESS

An imprint of Penguin Random House

PENGUIN BUSINESS

Penguin Business is an imprint of the Penguin Random House group of companies
whose addresses can be found at global.penguinrandomhouse.com

Published by Penguin Random House India Pvt. Ltd
4th Floor, Capital Tower 1, MG Road,
Gurugram 122 002, Haryana, India

First published in Portfolio by Penguin Random House India 2018
Published in Penguin Business by Penguin Random House India 2025

45 44 43 42 41 40

ISBN 9780143442479

Typeset in Aldine401 BT by MAP Systems, Bengaluru, India
Printed at Gopsons Papers Pvt. Ltd., Noida

www.penguin.co.in

*To the catalysts of my life—my parents, Meera,
Prerana, my family, my friends,
and Bharat and Anand*

Contents

PART III

Introduction

Success Needs a Catalyst

Igraduated with a degree in chemical engineering. Though I did not pursue a technical or an engineering career after that, some concepts from my graduation days have stayed with me. One such concept is how reactions are catalysed or the impact of the presence of a catalyst.

The basic concept is that the presence of a catalyst causes or accelerates a chemical reaction. In some cases, the ingredients are available, but the reaction does not happen spontaneously. It takes the catalyst to make it happen. In other words, the reaction has to be catalysed. There are many such examples around us in our daily life. E.g. automobile emissions contain carbon monoxide, which is highly dangerous. It has to be converted to carbon dioxide to make it less harmful. There is oxygen in the air, but it does not automatically react with this carbon monoxide to form carbon dioxide. It takes the catalytic converter fitted in automobiles for this reaction to occur. Another example is that of enzymes, which catalyse the digestive reactions in our body.

For a long time after my graduation, I continued to think of 'catalysts' and 'catalyse' as engineering terms. However, over many decades in the corporate world, I started to realize that even success at work and in life needs to be catalysed—it doesn't happen by itself. Many people have the ingredients for success, but they mistakenly assume that just the presence of these will guarantee success. Unfortunately, that is not the case; it needs a catalyst, which comes in the form of specific actions and efforts.

This notion has been in my head for a long time. I have also learnt from experience that success is the result of a holistic process. It is about catalysing a lot of reactions that most of us assume happen spontaneously. I have wanted to recount and share my experiences to help other people succeed using my learning. Towards this end, a few years ago, I built a module called 'Tee off with Mouli' (the name comes from my passion for golf) and started sharing it with the people I was working with, in sessions of about three hours each. I got a very good response and also some good feedback, which I used to further refine the module.

In the middle of 2016, I decided that I needed a break from work. I wanted to take a sabbatical. I was also keen that it should not be only about relaxation and fun but also about making significant social impact using my experience and learning. I spent time thinking about the best way of giving back to society. I had several ideas, including working with NGOs, but finally felt that none of these would give a high ROI (return on investment). I strongly believe that one must look for ROI in one's social efforts. Just because we give our time/money/knowledge does not mean it is making an impact. This does not mean that we stop giving our time/money/knowledge. My only suggestion is that each one of us try and invest it where it has the highest ROI. E.g. if you are a doctor and you want to make a social impact, perhaps the highest ROI for your social contribution is in trying to improve the health of the needy. A doctor could make an impact teaching maths to underprivileged children, but the ROI here would be lower than the ROI in healthcare. As I started thinking along these lines, it came to me—my highest ROI was going to be in helping people in the corporate sector achieve even greater success in their careers and lives. Their success would catalyse social impact and, over time, create employment and, in general, create a well-rounded, values-driven society.

As this became clear to me, I started to take 'Tee off with Mouli' to any company that was interested. In a four-month period, I took about thirty sessions of three hours each for over a thousand people at various companies. It was a part of my social mission and hence, I did not charge anything; my only condition was that the senior people should be personally involved in this process. As this unfolded, I started to get tremendous positive feedback for the sessions. Many people said that it was life-changing and that they wished they had received these insights earlier in their lives. Many of them urged me to convert this content into a book. Their belief was that it was too valuable, and it could have greater social impact if many more could access it. That, dear readers, is the inspiration for this book.

I named the module 'Tee off with Mouli' as it was more than just a catchy title. It was intended to be an inspiring analogy. Golf is not a popular sport, and so many people don't know much about it. The tee shot is the first shot in any hole when playing golf—you put a tee stick on the ground, place the ball on the tee and then hit it. That process is called teeing off or tee off in short. A well-hit tee shot is one of the most stirring spectacles—the ball flies, and can travel well over 250 yards. Consider a sixer in cricket, which travels about 80 yards, and a soaring goalkeeper's kick in football, which takes the ball about 60 yards. A tee shot is like three cricket sixes or four goal kicks in a row. The ball soars and soars, and takes forever to come down. My mission is to help people soar, achieve great heights and go very far, and that was the analogy that made me name the session 'Tee off with Mouli'. It was the mission of getting people to soar like the golf ball, high and long.

And that is what I hope every reader of this book will get—the inspiration to soar high and long, to achieve great success and a balanced life. I want the readers to understand that having the ingredients of success—education, IQ, EQ, hard work, a good job, etc.—does not mean that a person will automatically become successful. They have to understand what the catalysts for success are and make an effort to embed these catalysts in their work lives. Unfortunately, many people do not understand this and hence, often do not achieve the success for which they have the ingredients.

I do have an important disclaimer to make. This book is written from the lens of a practising manager, and is based on the insights I have gained into how to catalyse success. Hence, it is principally my point of view that I have put across; it has not necessarily been validated or proven. In many cases, I am simply presenting what I believe in. If your belief is different from mine, feel free to hold on to it. Please be aware that the contents of this book are not scientifically proven, but have been validated through the journey of my life and my work.

PART I

1

Real Individual Growth, the Catalyst for Success

In all my experiences and travels across the world, the one thing that has stood out is the hunger for success that most people have, Indians in particular. Often, that hunger for success is simplified by most people into a desire for success and growth in their careers. Success in life is equal to success in career is often the operating assumption of most people. In the latter portion of the book, I do try to give a more holistic dimension to success in life by including values, character and other related aspects. However, in the first half of the book, I focus primarily on giving people what they want—the keys to success at work.

I have a simple equation for career growth:

$$\text{Career growth} = \text{Real individual growth} \pm \text{Environmental aspects}$$

'Real individual growth' is the growth we experience in the duration of our careers—how much each one of us grows our knowledge, our skills, our judgement, our influence, our communication, etc. The second factor is 'environmental aspects', which covers things like the buoyancy of the job market, industry-related factors, relative availability of talent in your skill areas, etc.

Let me first cover the impact of environmental aspects on career growth. Our careers are typically forty years long. We start in our twenties and wind it up in our sixties. During these forty years, we will have both environmental tailwinds and headwinds in our careers. An example of a tailwind would be the times in your career when the job market is hyper-hot for the skills you have and there is a shortage of the skills you bring to the table. People tend to get jobs and salaries bigger than what they deserve, sometimes leading to short-lived growth 'bubbles'. Another example of a tailwind is when your boss quits the company, you are not yet fully ready to take on that role, but the company decides it would rather go with an insider and thus gives the job to you regardless. Such tailwinds are bound to support most of us in our careers at one time or the other.

Similarly, we have all also experienced headwinds in our careers. There are times when the economy is dragging, the job market is weak and there are very few opportunities for growth. Another example of a headwind is when you have been steadily getting ready for a big job, equipping yourself with the right experiences, apprenticing under the right leaders and preparing yourself for the opportunity, and when the opportunity comes, the company decides it wants new thinking and a change in strategy, and hence prefers to hire an outsider for the role as opposed to promoting an insider. You did nothing wrong, but the dice did not roll your way.

My experience is that in a forty-year career, the headwinds and the tailwinds balance each other out. You have to be a very lucky person for the tailwinds over forty years to be greater than the headwinds, and similarly, you have to be very unlucky for the headwinds to be greater than the tailwinds. For most people, the two balance out. Hence, going back to our career growth equation, this means that the environmental aspects will not be the deciding factor in driving career growth.

The catalyst of career growth tends to be real individual growth. Simply put, your career will grow only as much as you are able to grow as an individual and as a professional—what I call real individual growth. If you manage to grow your skills, your knowledge, your decision-making ability, your judgement, your influence on others, your communication skills, etc., then you will experience career growth. Career growth is directly proportional to, and is a function of, real individual growth. If you stop pushing yourself at any stage, your career growth also comes to a screeching halt.

Hence the equation of career growth can be simplified to:

Career growth = Real individual growth

One way I like to state this is through the expression 'You get what you deserve'. Far too often in our careers, we focus on the getting part of it. We focus on getting the promotion, getting the new job, getting career growth. We do not focus on deserving more by increasing our capabilities, our skills and so on. In a career, you get only what you deserve. It is useful to remember what is in our hands, and focus on deserving more and driving our real individual growth.

My belief is that if we stop focusing on career growth and put all our energies into real individual growth, towards deserving more, then we will experience greater career growth. It keeps our focus firmly on what we can influence, working on ourselves, rather than distracting ourselves with the thought of career growth all the time—which can cause anxiety and result in poor choices. To use a sporting analogy, if you want to become the captain of the team, you must focus on hitting the next ball out of the ground. If you continuously keep hitting the balls out of the ground, there is a chance that one day, you will be the captain. If you are desperately trying to become the captain, there will be so much anxiety that you will stop hitting the ball out of the park, which will then diminish your chances of achieving your goal.

There is a similar thought in Indian philosophy—'*Tu karm kar, phal ki chinta mat kar*'. Loosely translated, it means, 'Focus on the deeds, don't worry about the results.' I am sure similar thoughts exist in all cultures and religions. This particular one comes from the Bhagavad Gita and was spoken by Lord Krishna. For a while, I used to be intrigued on whether it is even possible to practise that philosophy, to focus only on the deeds and not bother about the results. Aren't results important? How practical is it to not bother about the results and only bother about the deeds? It took me many conversations and careful reflection to get my own thinking and understanding on this sorted out. My understanding now is—the probability of getting the result you want increases when you stop thinking about the results and start focusing on the deeds for getting that result. Going back to our sporting analogy, if you want to become the captain of the cricket team, then the deeds towards that result are scoring consistently, becoming a leader among your fellow players, understanding the strategies of the game, etc. If you focus on these deeds, then you maximize the probability of becoming the captain, but if you focus on becoming the captain without focusing on the deeds, you actually reduce your probability of attaining your goal.

I believe career growth is something like that—the more you focus on it, the less effective it is. Instead the more you focus on the deeds which lead to career growth, which is real individual growth, the more likely you are to have positive career growth. If you stop thinking about career growth—the next job, the next promotion—and instead be relentless in growing yourself and becoming continuously better—improving your knowledge, skills, judgement, influence, communication, etc.—the more career growth you will experience. Real individual growth, my friends, is the catalyst, the 'deeds' for the result called career growth.

So what does real individual growth mean and how does one drive it? This is where *Catalyst*, the book, comes in. One of the most common misconceptions is that real individual growth happens by itself. Most people assume that if they work hard and spend years at work, then they are growing their skills, knowledge and capabilities. That is a misconception. Time and hard work alone do not drive real individual growth; it needs to be catalysed. There are four core areas where this has to be done, and this book will cover these areas in detail.

Experience Needs a Catalyst

The first area is that of our learning model. Our simplistic assumption is that if we spend enough time at work and work hard, then we are learning and gaining experience. This is fundamentally wrong. Time spent at work is not equal to experience. If that were true, all those with the same amount of work experience would be equally successful. Experience is not gained automatically; it has to be catalysed.

Higher Productivity Needs a Catalyst

The next assumption is in the area of personal productivity. We assume that as we keep growing, our productivity keeps increasing as well. This assumption is wrong. It has to be catalysed; it will not grow by itself. Many people get to senior levels or even higher levels and fail, not because of a lack of capability, but because their productivity has not grown by itself over the years. Now they are caught, as they face the complex multi-stakeholder, multitasking environment of senior roles requiring higher personal productivity—the improvement that they have not catalysed. Productivity does not increase by itself; it has to be catalysed.

Catalysts for Career Management

The next area that requires a catalyst is that of career management. Our simplistic assumption is that if we succeed in the first halves of our careers, we will automatically succeed in the second halves as well. This assumption is also incorrect. The second half needs the catalysts of specific efforts and actions. Let's take two people with roughly similar qualifications and compare their career success after they have retired. Let us assume for a moment that one has been very successful while the other has been moderately successful. You will find that the bulk of their success difference developed only in the second halves of their careers. At the end of the first halves, they would have been equally successful. Most people are successful in the first halves of their careers, but very few in the second. Career success in the second half doesn't happen by itself based on success in the first half; it has to be catalysed.

Life and Values as Catalysts for Success

The next area is that of the work–life interaction. Another simplistic assumption we make is that work has a huge impact on life, hence the focus on areas like work–life balance, stress management and so on. In my opinion, the impact of work on life is lower than the impact of life on work. How we lead our lives has a huge impact on how successful we are at work and, indeed, in life. There are a set of things which can have a tremendous positive catalysing impact on our long-term success at work. Success at work doesn't happen by just slogging at work; it is catalysed by the way we live our lives.

Career growth is driven by real individual growth. And real individual growth does not happen simply by working hard and spending years gathering experience. How you can catalyse your real individual growth is the objective of this book, and the focus of the following chapters. While there are three distinct sections in the book—the first on experience-building, the second on career management and the third on life and values—it is not necessary to see them in a sequential way. You need not work first on experience, then on career management and then on life and values. It is fine to work on all of them at the same time. Please do read the book with this in mind.

2

Time Spent at Work Does
Not Equal Experience

Interviewer: Tell me, what experience do you have?
Candidate: I have fourteen years' experience doing financial accounting.

Conversations like the one above play out all the time in the corporate world. These perpetuate the myth that experience is equal to time and can be measured in years. Nothing could be further from the truth.

One of the foundational drivers of real individual growth is experience. All of us know that experience is important. It is critical for success in careers. We all agree that we must gain 'good experience' in the relevant areas to become successful. And we are willing to invest our time, the most valuable and limited resource we have, in getting it. Experience is important for success, folks—in fact, it is super important—and yet most of us have an incomplete and inadequate understanding of it.

I often start my training sessions by asking somebody in the audience, 'How many years of experience do you have walking?' It often draws a chuckle. Then I follow up with, 'How many years of experience do you have sleeping?' and the chuckle turns to laughter. Then there's usually a serious question: 'How many years of experience do you have in finance or sales or marketing or HR?' and there is a serious answer, no laughter. Why is it that we do not consider the time spent in activities like walking and sleeping as 'experience'? How are we so sure that the time spent at work on sales or marketing or production automatically becomes experience, while that spent walking or sleeping does not? Time does not become experience by itself, even at work; it has to be catalysed.

The reason we believe that the time spent walking and sleeping is not experience is because we perform these activities in a highly mechanical/thoughtless way. We do not have an active learning model associated with walking; we do not say the more we walk, the better we become at walking. It feels like we walk roughly the same way we used to years ago, with no significant improvement over time. The bulk of our learning in walking happened in the first few years of our childhood. We learnt rapidly, there was a learning model, and the more we walked, the better we became. Then the learning stopped as we started doing it mechanically/thoughtlessly.

Having established that time spent walking is not experience, except during childhood, now let me establish that the contrary is also true. Walking is not 'experience' for you and me, but for an athlete who participates in the Olympics walking event with his or her eyes set on the gold medal, it surely would be counted as experience. They obviously have a learning model associated with walking, which helps them get continuously better. Similarly, take the case of someone who is a professional model and walks the ramp. They spend hours trying to perfect their walk. So walking is 'experience' for both the Olympic athlete and the model, but not for you and me. This establishes that it is not the activity that determines whether something counts as experience or not, but the way in which it is done. The presence of a learning model as a catalyst determines whether the activity becomes experience or not. For both the Olympic athlete and us, the activity is the same—walking. But the former catalyses that activity into experience with a learning model, while we don't. The same can happen at work too.

One of the greatest myths of our times is that experience at work is measured in units of time. Time is not an accurate measure of experience. E.g. if you are hiring and you see two candidates, one with ten years of experience and the other with fifteen years of experience, your automatic assumption is that the latter has greater experience. What if the person with fifteen years of experience worked as if they were walking/sleeping at work, while the person with ten years of experience worked in a highly learning-oriented way, catalysing their work into experience? The number of years of experience a person has at work is a measure of just that—how much time they have spent at work. It does not measure how powerful their learning during that period was, and it is not a measure of the experience they have built in the process.

If experience is not equal to time, then how should we understand and define it? Let us go back to our hiring analogy. Our assumption is that, given the same situation in the future, the candidate with fifteen years of experience will do better than the one with ten years. Hence, our implicit understanding of experience is about how it enables us to respond to future situations. Thus, the purpose of experience for us is not to measure what we have done in the past, but to use it to do better in the future.

Therein lies the nub of the issue, which is how we should define experience. Should we define it as what we have done in the past or should we define it as what it has built in us for us to do better in the future? I fundamentally disagree with the paradigm of defining it based on time spent in the past. There is only one purpose to it, which is how it enables us to do better in the future.

I like to define experience as the algorithm that we have built in ourselves doing what we have done. You could also think of it as the software in you, the program in you. As we do stuff, we are continuously adding to the software, the program, trying to make it better, and that algorithm/software/program is our experience. That is what responds to situations in the future.

Hence, put simply, the more powerful the algorithm, the better the response to situations in the future. This means that the more experienced person is one whose algorithm is stronger, not necessarily one who has spent more years or done more of the activity. The purpose of the time spent and the activity done is to build the algorithm, to make it stronger over time. Any time spent or activity done that does not add to the algorithm is not experience.

One of the greatest success factors at work, therefore, is our ability to convert time and activity into experience (the algorithm). My view is that what differentiates more successful people from less successful people is the effectiveness with which they convert time into experience. It does not happen by itself; it needs a catalyst. The rest of this chapter describes that catalyst.

TMRR: The Catalyst for Converting Time into Experience

Let us go back to our example of the athlete in the Olympic walking event. We agreed that walking is not experience for you and me but it is for an athlete. What an athlete does to convert that activity into experience, when you and I can't, will help us understand the catalyst required for converting time and activity into experience.

The first thing the athlete does is to set a target for the activity. He or she has a target of, let's say, three hours and forty-two minutes for a 50 km walk. Then the athlete measures the actual performance against that target. Let's say the athlete actually clocked three hours and forty-nine minutes in the race. He or she then reviews the actual performance against the target, and tries to understand the reasons for the performance. In this case, the athlete might analyse different segments of the race, say, the beginning, the middle and the end, and might conclude that the ending was poor, which means their stamina was poor and hence they need endurance training. Or the athlete could review different terrains and conclude that the performance in the uphill section of the race was poor, which could mean that the length of the stride going uphill was shorter than required, which could be because of the hamstring muscle not being strong enough. Based on such analysis, the person would build a plan to work on performance improvement. The presence of the learning model and the will to want to improve—these are the two drivers that the athlete has in walking that you and I don't. Hence, it becomes experience for the athlete, but a mindless activity for us.

To summarize, having a target for the activity, measuring the actual performance and then reviewing the performance to understand why it was the way it was—that is the learning model that we need to employ in each and every activity to catalyse and convert our time and activity into experience, the algorithm. I call this the Target, Measure and Review (TMR) model—the most effective learning model at work. It sounds simple, but the tragedy is that most people usually do not employ a learning model at work, and hence do not convert their time into experience.

In my judgement, half the time people spend at work, they do not employ a learning model, they do not have a target for the activity, they certainly have poor measurement systems and they do not review their performance to understand the reasons for it. People might find it difficult to accept that there is no TMR model in play for over half their time. This is because the companies have targets, which are often passed on to employees through annual goal-setting, incentive processes and other such activities. Hence people believe that they have a target for every minute they spend at work. But let us dive deeper into this and analyse the truth.

Let us say Mr A is a sales manager in a reputed firm. Sales is a highly measurable function—there are targets, a measuring of actual sales and a consequent review. Hence, Mr A could be thinking, TMR for me is an automatic occurrence—I have a target for everything, I measure my actuals and I review the performance all the time. So all my time must be getting converted into experience. However, the question we are asking is not 'Does your role have a target?' but 'Are you converting your time into experience?' To do that, it is not enough for your role to have targets. What is important is that every unit of time that you spend at work has a target. Hence, the question for Mr A is not whether he has a sales target, but whether he has a target for every hour of time he has spent on an activity, and whether he does the TMR for each hour and each day. Let us say Mr A spends 5 per cent of his time on hiring people for his team. Does that 5 per cent have an effective TMR? This activity has an indirect contribution to the sales performance and hence one could argue that the TMR for this 5 per cent also happens through targeting, measuring and reviewing the sales numbers. However, that linkage is indirect and not a direct TMR of the activity and time spent in hiring people. The fact is, Mr A probably did not have a target for his performance in hiring people, did not measure how he performed and did not review the reasons for that performance. The TMR for the sales performance does not make up for the absence of the TMR for the 5 per cent of time spent on hiring. There is, therefore, a question mark over whether Mr A indeed catalysed that 5 per cent time into experience and improved his algorithm. My guess would be no.

A similar activity on which Mr A spends a lot of time is market and customer visits—again, a situation in which time is often not converted into experience. This is because of the mistaken belief that targeting, measuring and reviewing the sales numbers at the end of the month/year is a fair way of measuring and learning from each customer visit. However, the question we are again asking is about Mr A converting time into experience, and that time is not spent on a monthly/annual basis, but hour by hour, visit by visit. If Mr A wants to convert time into experience, he has to have the TMR process for each customer visit and not assume that the TMR for the month/year is a proxy for that.

The key thing, folks, is that we are talking about converting time into experience, and time at work is not spent at an aggregate level for each activity, but is spent by the hour, by the day. That is why TMR at an aggregate level, for the quarter or for the year, does not help. The really effective people understand intuitively that they have to learn every hour and every day, and have a catalyst for converting time into experience on an hourly, daily basis. Hence I believe that most people spend over 50 per cent of their time at work as if they were walking or sleeping. They do not convert it into experience and they do not use every hour to improve their algorithm.

There is a second reason why most of us do not convert time at work into experience. That is because we mistakenly believe that organizational processes are equal to individual processes. I have often heard people say, 'I have a very demanding boss who reviews everything I do every day, so my experience building is happening automatically, thanks to my boss.' Yes, there is a role your company and your bosses play in building your experience, your algorithm, and we will discuss it in greater detail in chapter 7. However, let us examine whether that alone can help in individual experience-building. To understand that we must understand the intent of the boss in reviewing you every day. It is mostly to ensure that the desired results are produced for the company. Your boss does not review you with the intention of improving your algorithm for the time you spent at work that day. Yes, there is some overlap between a review for the company and your algorithm improvement, but the review for the desired results is not fully effective in converting time into experience for individuals.

Let me give another example to explain this further. Let us assume that you are part of a team that executed an important project for your company. Like all important projects, this one would also have had a target, measurements and active project reviews. In a way, there is a very active project TMR process. Would that process substitute for the individual TMR process and be effective in converting your time spent on that project into experience? I do not think so. Let me describe some scenarios and reasons for that.

The project might have been very successful for the company, but does that mean it was a great experience for you? That would depend on how effective your contribution was in making that project a success, and how effective your personal learning model was when making that contribution. Just because the project was a great success does not mean it was a great experience for you. Now let us assume that the project was a failure for the company. Does that mean it was a poor experience for you? It need not have been. If your contribution was effective and you had a very active personal TMR learning model for the time you spent on that project, it is likely to be a great experience builder for you.

The project TMR process is the learning model the company puts into place for itself, something I call the organizational experience-building process. This can build the organizational experience and algorithm, but that does not mean that every member of that project team gets the same experience out of it. Each team member builds a different experience based on how effective their personal TMR was for the time they spent on the project.

The Fourth R

To ensure that the personal TMR is highly effective in such situations, I advocate adding a fourth R to TMR and making it TMRR. This fourth R is 'Reflection'. And I like people to reflect using a very specific question: 'What could *I* have done *better*?' As is obvious from the emphasis, the two most important words in that question are 'I' and 'better'. The reason for this is the purpose of reflection, which is to understand how to add to your experience and thus build your algorithm. To ensure that, you should focus on the 'I'. If you reflect on the question 'What could have been done better on this project?' without the I, then it will generate answers which improve the overall organizational experience and it might not be specific to you. But if the question is 'What could I have done better in this project?' then the answers will strengthen your experience and your algorithm.

The second critical word in that question is 'better'. It does sound like a negative word. But the question is not 'What did I do well?' The reason for the focus on 'better' again goes on to show why we are doing this reflection. Even if you have done well and achieved a lot of success in the project, only when you reflect on what you could have done better will it add to the algorithm. Only this will help you build the experience that will enable you to respond to situations in the future better than how you are responding today.

The TMR process is the crucial learning model that converts time into experience. Often, however, when people work in a company, organizational TMR process overlaps with the individual TMR process, and hence reduces the effectiveness of the individuals converting time into experience. To make up for that, I recommend the catalyst of reflection. When you add the fourth R, when TMR becomes TMRR, it will complete the process of you converting your time into your experience, distinct from the company converting its time into its experience.

An Example of TMRR

I recently interacted with a young manager who had just completed a project. I said, 'Let me help you catalyse that time you spent on the project and convert it into experience. Let us start with the question "What could I have done better in that project?"' The young manager gave me a set of answers, but I felt they lacked depth. So I worded my question differently. 'If you started the project again, with all the learning you have now, having done it once, what would you do differently?' A clearer list emerged of what could have been done better. And then I asked another question, 'Why could you not anticipate these areas right up front and do the project even better the first time? Were they impossible to anticipate and could they be known only after the project's completion? Or was it that you failed to anticipate what was possible to anticipate?' You can imagine the quality of reflection that is required to answer that question, and how that would build experience out of the time spent on this project. The young manager spent three months doing the project, but did not spend the few hours required to convert these three months into experience. A series of reflection questions like 'What could I have done better?' is crucial for truly converting time spent into valuable experience. If that is not done, then it is not time spent, but alas, time wasted.

If there is one thing you take from this book and practise regularly, I hope it is reflection. It is a catalyst that is capable of significantly growing your experience and hence driving real individual growth. Just this one thing, I promise, will make you more successful in your career. The key truth, however, is that most of us will struggle to practise it regularly. We know it is good for us, but we may not be able to do it with regularity and consistency. Even if we have good intentions, like dieting, exercising and reading regularly, we do not convert these into behaviour and action. And I am afraid that even something as important as the TMRR process, a catalyst that can single-handedly transform how successful you are in your career, might remain a good intention with most of you.

Building the Reflection Habit

What, then, is the key to converting intention to lasting behaviour and action? I believe that key is building a habit. Good intent gets converted to action when it gets ingrained as a habit. Most of you did not forget to brush your teeth today, even if you slept late last night, because it is ingrained as a habit. If we could ingrain reflection as a habit, like brushing our teeth, then we would reflect every day, and we would build greater experience and achieve much more success in our careers.

The key to building a habit is persistence in the first 15–30 reps (repetitions) of building the habit. Today, brushing our teeth is an effortless habit for us, but for our parents, who ensured that this became a habit for us, it meant chasing us when we were children and ensuring that we did it. They forced us, induced us and convinced us to do it every day till it became a habit. The habit of reflection is similar; it requires us to show the same persistence in the initial phase till it becomes an ingrained habit. One way of ensuring a habit is through the concept of anchoring. If our parents had taught us that it was acceptable to brush our teeth any time we wanted during the day, not necessarily first thing in the morning, then maybe, on some days, we would forget to do it. But because the habit is anchored in the occasion of waking up in the morning, there is a much greater chance that we practise it every day. Similarly, if we could anchor the reflection habit, then there is a much greater chance it will be practised every day. My own anchor for the reflection habit is at the end of the work day, when I get into my car to go back home from work. I spend the first fifteen minutes reflecting, answering the question 'What could I have done better?' It is now an anchored habit—every evening after work, when I am in the car, I automatically start to reflect, and it happens every day without fail. I do have the privilege of having a chauffeur. For those of you who drive, it might not be safe to reflect while driving, so do find a different anchor—maybe the evening drive or ride back, maybe fifteen minutes on either side of the lunch break, maybe just before you sleep. Whatever the occasion, anchoring is going to make it happen every day, and if it happens every day, then you have a significantly higher chance of increasing your experience, growing your algorithm and being more successful.

Unleash the Catalyst

1. Time is the single greatest investment and resource you put into your career. However, this time is not automatically converted into the experience and algorithm that will drive your real individual growth and career success.
2. To convert time into experience, you require a catalyst, and that catalyst is TMRR: Target, Measure, Review and Reflect.
3. To make this effective, you must build an anchored habit of reflection on the question 'What could *I* have done *better*?'

The single greatest difference I have seen between more successful people and less successful people is their ability to catalyse and convert time into experience. Hence, it is worth all the effort that you can put in to adopt the catalyst of TMRR in your work and develop an anchored habit of daily reflection.

3

Maximize Learning Cycles

I have witnessed the professional journeys of several successful people. One common aspect in their journeys is that they have all had the opportunity to be an integral, end-to-end part of a very important project or initiative or transformation. Additionally, that project or initiative seems to have played a significant role in building the experiential algorithm for these successful individuals and has contributed disproportionately to their learning and real individual growth.

In my work life, I was involved early on in a project for creating a full, new segment for my company. This involved studying the market, identifying the opportunity, formulating an entry strategy and developing the product, followed by launching the product and taking necessary action to build that segment. I was involved with this project for close to three-and-a-half years, and I learnt the end-to-end game of creating a segment from its infancy.

This was an important project for the company, and companies often use terms like 'project' or 'transformation' or 'initiative' for such efforts. For me, as an individual, it was more than just a project, it was more than just building a new segment. It was an extraordinary experience-building process with huge learning. A project of this kind impacts experience, learning and real individual growth. Hence, from an individual perspective, instead of calling it a 'project', I like to use the term 'learning cycle'. Each of these projects or initiatives represents a potential learning cycle for individuals.

A learning cycle is any project, initiative or transformation that happens routinely in companies. E.g. a new product launch. That learning cycle starts with the process of identifying the need for a new product, building a business proposal for it, going through the product development cycle, including prototyping, researching and testing as required, building the manufacturing or service capabilities required and then launching it into the market. The learning cycle ends after the launch, when the new product has stabilized in the market, and corrective action, if required, has been taken. This whole thing, end-to-end, is one learning cycle.

Any major project or initiative represents a potential learning cycle. It could be the conceptualization and execution of a major organizational structure and culture change, it could be an initiative for significant new distribution creation, it could be a project for cost reduction and fundamental transformation of the end-to-end supply chain or it could be the launch of a new enterprise software. Each of these initiatives or projects, and others of this nature, represents a significant potential learning cycle for individuals to grow their experience and drive real individual growth.

Let us first understand the relationship between TMRR, described in the earlier chapter, and the learning cycle. The TMRR is the 'how' of building experience and real individual growth, while the learning cycle is the 'what' of it—as in on what opportunity do you apply the TMRR. Both create a huge impact as the cumulative learning based on these two aspects is multiplicative. The learning cycle represents the potential of experience-building in a project/initiative, while TMRR is a process by which you extract that experience-building opportunity. An analogy to understand that would be to visualize an artist and a performance opportunity. The learning cycle is equivalent to the size, scale and stature of the stage on which the artist performs; the greater the size of the audience, the greater the prestige of the stage—the greater the opportunity for the artist to create an impact. Having said that, that opportunity for creating impact will be realized only if the artist performs well. How well the artist performs is the equivalent of TMRR for experience-building. Hence, the cumulative impact the artist can create is a combination of the scale/stature of the stage and the performance of the artist. If both are great, the artist creates a tremendous impact. However, if either of them is small, then the cumulative impact is significantly reduced because it is a multiplicative equation. Hence, a great performance on a small stage does not create great impact for the artist. Equally, a poor performance on a great stage also does not create impact for the artist. Only when both the stage and the performance are great does the impact become great.

That is how one needs to think of the learning cycle and the TMRR experience-building process. The learning cycle represents the stage—the more significant the learning cycle, the greater the opportunity to drive real individual growth and build up experience. The TMRR is equivalent to the artist's performance—how much experience you extract out of the learning cycle will be driven by how well you applied the TMRR process on the learning cycle.

Hence, if you want to drive real individual growth in the quest for success, then you have to maximize both the size and scale of the learning cycles you participate in and the extraction of experience through effective TMRR. And when I observed more successful people in their careers, that is precisely what I found they did.

I have observed that more successful people do these two things better than less successful people:

1. Successful people seemed to have participated in more major learning cycles than those who are less successful.
2. Successful people seemed to have extracted more experience and real individual growth out of the learning cycles they participated in than less successful people.

Make Major Learning Cycles Happen

I'm starting with the first observation: Successful people seemed to have participated in more major learning cycles than those who are less successful. The more I engage with and observe successful people, the clearer it is to me that each one of them has had the opportunity to be an integral, end-to-end part of a major learning cycle in their careers. In many cases, these people were responsible for leading those initiatives, not just participating in them, and hence the impact of the learning cycle was even more profound. In some cases, very early on in their careers, by sheer good luck, serendipity or being in the right place at the right time, they got drafted into key initiatives that proved to be major learning cycles, and hence had a transformational impact on their experience, real individual growth and consequent career success. Some of them asked for and became part of a major initiative even if they were originally not a part of it, and that initiative became a major learning cycle for them. In some cases, they developed a powerful new initiative or transformation as a part of their day job and went on to lead it, and that created a powerful learning cycle for them that fundamentally transformed their growth and career. Whichever way it happened, the fact remained that major learning cycles were a very important catalyst in the success of these people.

To quote a real situation, many years ago, I had a high-quality brand manager working in my team. That was the time I initiated a project on fundamental brand transformation, going to the very core of what the brand stands for, and worked with a brand consulting company. In the initial phase, the brand manager worked with me on that project, and then I happened to leave the company. Hence, he got the opportunity to lead the project, which he did with great success, completely reinventing the brand. It was a three-year learning cycle of brand transformation, with initial tutelage from me, and then independent charge. That person has gone on to become extraordinarily successful in his career, garnering much global acclaim, and I have no doubt that the brand transformation learning cycle in the formative stages of his career was pivotal in building the experience algorithm on which his subsequent success was built.

This and many other such examples made it apparent to me that if you want more than average success in your career, you must not only do your daily nine-to-five job but also seek an opportunity to participate in a major project, initiative or transformation that can be the success-creating learning cycle that your career needs. For many of these people, the major learning cycle happened by chance. Yet, something that happened by chance had a profound impact on their professional success. The question then is, can you make a major learning cycle happen in your career, preferably in the earlier stages, or are you going to depend on chance?

What does it take to engender a major learning cycle in your career? There are many ways to make this happen. First and foremost, keep your eyes and ears open. Such initiatives abound in any company. See if any of these fit your skills, if you can make a contribution to any of them, and then try and become a part of that initiative. You can do this by asking, volunteering or putting yourself in a place where that initiative needs you. Another way is to conceptualize a transformational initiative as a part of your day job, and then lead that and make it a major learning cycle. E.g. if you are in marketing, you can conceptualize a significant new product opportunity, which the company finds so interesting that they give you the mandate and the resources to lead that project end-to-end, making it a big learning cycle. Or if you are heading a factory, you can conceptualize a significant capacity expansion opportunity and that becomes a major initiative for the company and a major learning cycle for you. Or if you are an IT professional, you can conceptualize a significant artificial intelligence–based decision-making process that can automate many manual decisions, and then you get to lead that initiative, making a milestone learning cycle for your career. Or if you are an HR professional, you can conceptualize a new way of incentivizing employees and then lead that initiative in end-to-end implementation, making it a rewarding learning cycle for you.

Whichever way it happens, whether you conceptualize it or participate in an already conceptualized initiative, the opportunity to be a part of it, which can be a major learning cycle, is a key catalyst in a successful career. It is sad to meet people who are capable, but for whatever reason have never been part of a major transformational learning cycle opportunity, and hence have not experienced the career success they had the potential for. If you get lucky and get to participate in a big learning cycle, that is fantastic. But if you are not lucky and a major learning cycle does not come your way, then you have to make one happen in your career—it is absolutely imperative as a catalyst for success.

Get More out of It

The second observation I made was: Successful people seem to get more out of the learning cycles they participate in than less successful people. So while the first observation was about the opportunity to participate in a learning cycle, the second observation is about what you get out of it. Many people get to participate in major learning cycles, but are unable to get real individual growth out of it. Hence, it is not correct to assume that just participating in a learning cycle is enough to extract experience and real individual growth. That experience and real individual growth has to be catalysed. Two people participating in the same initiative—the same learning cycle—can end up with very different experiences and real individual growth, depending on whether they catalysed the learning opportunity or not.

So what does it take to catalyse experience and real individual growth from the opportunity to participate in a major learning cycle? There are four things I have observed successful people do, and I would like to describe them in the following paragraphs.

Effective TMRR Application

The first observation goes back to the TMRR described in the previous chapter and how well that is applied on the major learning cycle. The more effective the TMRR application on the learning cycle, the more experience a person extracts out of it. And the key to that, as described in the previous chapter, is to distinguish the organizational TMR from the individual TMR by adding the R of reflection. A major learning cycle for the individual often also represents a major project or initiative for the firm. Hence, the firm always has very rigorous target, measure and review processes being applied on the project. Because of the rigour of the TMR process for the project, many people mistakenly assume that it is enough, that the firm's TMR process on the project is creating experience for you. It is not—you have to focus on extracting experience for yourself by adding the last R of reflection, based on the question 'What could I have done better in this learning cycle opportunity that I got?' Successful people were clearly better at applying the TMRR process in a major learning cycle and creating experience for themselves.

Be at Your Best

The second thing that successful people seem to instinctively do is seize the opportunity of a major learning cycle by increasing the intensity of their engagement and prioritizing the learning cycle over the other activities they do on a daily basis. Again, going back to our analogy, great artists are those who are able to raise their performance much above their mean when they get a big stage. These artists instinctively realize that they have to be at their very best on the big stage—the daily normal won't do. Similarly, successful people seem to realize that major learning cycles represent a fantastic opportunity to gain experience and drive a steep jump in real individual growth. Hence, they increase the intensity of their engagement and prioritize the learning cycle in their work lives. They try to be at their best in a major learning cycle. They do this by increasing the extent of time they spend on the learning cycle, being at their best in terms of concentration, creativity and communication and being ultra-disciplined on the TMRR execution for themselves. Less successful people, on the contrary, seem to not realize that a particular initiative represents a major learning cycle. They engage with it as if it were just another regular thing they did at work and simply do not catalyse the opportunity that the learning cycle represents for them. The catalyst here is the intensity of engagement and prioritization, and the presence or absence of it determines what different people extract out of a major learning cycle.

Broaden the Lens

The third thing that successful people seem to differ in, beyond the intensity of engagement, is how broad their engagement is on major learning cycles. On a day-to-day basis, most people engage with issues at work by asking 'What is my role in it?' Often, we limit our contribution to what is required for the role. E.g. if you are an HR professional and somebody engages with you on a business initiative, you tend to restrict yourself to the HR part of the business initiative, i.e., the breadth of your engagement with that initiative is from the lens of your role and expertise only. What successful people seem to do in a major learning cycle is realize that it has high potential for driving their real individual growth and broaden their engagement beyond the scope of their role and expertise. They make an effort to engage holistically with that initiative. They also broaden their TMRR to beyond their lens. The question they ask themselves is, 'What could I have done better to make the project succeed holistically?' In contrast, less successful people keep their engagement narrow, limited to their lens, even in a major learning cycle, and the question they tend to ask themselves is something like, 'What could I have done better in this project on HR issues?'

Be the Thought Leader

The fourth thing that successful people seem to do in major learning cycles is to understand that project leadership is different from thought leadership. As mentioned, major learning cycles more often than not also happen to be important initiatives and projects for organizations. Successful people seem to instinctively realize that these represent an opportunity to contribute and learn beyond the usual. One way to maximize the learning value of a major learning cycle is to try and contribute at the thought leadership level to the project. In these initiatives, organizations are focused on getting the best thoughts, irrespective of where they come from, and when you push yourself to contribute at the thought leadership level, you maximize your learning from the learning cycle. You are able to assess your ability to operate at a higher level, the things you do well at that level and the things you need to improve to one day be the leader of a major learning cycle. Trying to operate at a level higher than your organizational position in a major learning cycle is a fantastic way to maximize the learning value of that cycle.

Unleash the Catalyst

Learning cycles are important catalysts for real individual growth. Learning cycles and TMRR operate in tandem to build your algorithm. The learning cycle is the 'what', the stage, the initiative from which you learn, and the TMRR is the process by which you extract the learning, the 'how'. Experience-building happens only when both are strong.

1. Successful people have participated in major learning cycles, and these have often happened relatively early in their careers. For you to succeed, you have to similarly participate in a major learning cycle, and if one does not come your way in the normal course of

things, then you must try and create the opportunity
yourself.

2. Successful people also extract the maximum out
    of the opportunity to participate in major learning
    cycles. They do this by effective implementation of
    the TMRR process, being at their best in the learning
    cycle, broadening their lens of engagement beyond
    just their functional and domain areas and operating
    at a level of thought leadership irrespective of their
    organizational level.

4

Improve Personal Productivity

Many years ago, I had a very capable individual working for me, somebody whom I thought very highly of, the kind you proclaim as 'excellent'. When a very senior position opened up, I grabbed the chance to elevate that person to that senior role. After a year, much to my dismay, things did not work out and I had to actually move that person from that role to a less challenging one. I reflected on the whys of it and realized that while the person had all the necessary skills and capabilities for the role—while he had a well-developed experience algorithm—he did not possess the necessary productivity to make a complex role work. He could not handle the multitasking the complex role required—the fact that many things have to be done at the same time and you have to be on top of all of them—could not decide which meetings to spend time on, which issues needed long deliberations, which issues should not be allowed to take more than five minutes, and so on. None of these were capability issues. If there were forty-eight hours in a day, that person had all the tools and wherewithal to succeed. But there are only twenty-four hours in a day, and that is where productivity comes in.

That episode taught me that success is a partnership of the experience algorithm and productivity. The algorithm is your ability to respond to a situation and get to the right answer; it is the ability to generate solutions to complex problems. In a way, the experience algorithm is the summary of your capabilities. That summary of capabilities has to be put to productive use to be able to finally create value and a favourable output. The output, then, is a multiplication of the algorithm and the productivity used in employing it. We have all seen different kinds of people. There are people who are highly capable and dazzle with insights, strategic thinking and knowledge, but at times they leave you exasperated by their lack of output and their inability to get things done and manage complexity. These are the people who are often labelled as high potential, but are yet to fire fully. They possess a high-quality algorithm but are poor on productivity. Then there are those who are moderate on capability, cannot create breakthrough solutions or strategies—in effect, have a moderately developed algorithm, but seem to get things done when told what to do, follow up diligently and are very disciplined about timelines, commitments, etc. Such people are often referred to loosely as the 'doers'. They are high on productivity but moderate on the algorithm.

Real high performers, those who achieve exceptional success, are those who are good at both. They have a highly developed algorithm which they employ with the highest productivity and hence are able to deliver both high quality and high quantity of output, making them highly successful in their careers. Such people are few and far between. If you want the highest level of success in your career, you have to aim for that high bar of both, a fantastic algorithm representing the summary of your capabilities and excellent productivity to convert that algorithm into output. Productivity is the means by which you convert your algorithm into output.

Most people who want to succeed do seem to realize the need to grow their algorithm/capabilities as a necessary prerequisite for success. I describe it using the phrase 'experience algorithm'. These people might not describe it the same way, but they all understand that if they have to achieve higher success, then they have to continuously grow their capabilities. There is a high degree of awareness that success requires capabilities, and that if I have to be successful, I have to make an active effort to grow my algorithm, or whatever words I use to describe it. However, interestingly, there is not the same degree of self-awareness about the need to grow productivity, and so there is often no effort put into increasing it. This is one of the most important mistakes people make, and is often the reason they don't achieve the full success they otherwise can.

The reason for this lack of effort in growing one's productivity is two-pronged. The first is the lack of self-awareness—as I mentioned above, most people are aware that to succeed, they have to grow their skills and capabilities, their algorithm, but they don't realize that it is equally important to grow their productivity. The second reason is the mistaken assumption that productivity grows by itself—the thought that if you work hard every day, if you keep achieving results, your productivity will grow by itself. It is the same myth that I pointed out in the context of experience—the mistaken assumption that if you keep working hard and putting in time, your experience is building up by itself. The same myth is prevalent to an even higher degree in the context of productivity. No, folks, productivity does not grow by itself; it has to be catalysed to grow.

In this chapter, I want to deal with these two issues: first, to make you aware that you need to improve your productivity, and second, to show you some techniques by which you can catalyse the growth of your productivity.

The 'Why' of Productivity

Why do you need to grow your productivity? Why is it so important for long-term career success? As people go up the corporate ladder, get to higher positions, here is what happens. They must have built up the higher order algorithm and capabilities to succeed at the higher level, so let us assume that is the case. But is that enough? As they go higher, the demands of the job also rise—no company gives you a higher order job, higher title and higher pay without having a higher expectation of output from you. You don't go higher with the ask being the same. To deliver that higher ask, let's say you have built up the higher order algorithm. But apart from that, you also need more time and energy to meet that higher order ask. Unfortunately, as we all know, time is a constant at twenty-four hours a day. I always say, the only thing common between a watchman and a chairman is twenty-four hours a day. If somebody progresses from being a watchman to a chairman—and I do wish everybody such great success in their careers— they have to deal with the fact that they have to meet the requirements of being a chairman with the same twenty-four hours they had as a watchman. As you get to senior levels, two things change: first, the complexity of the problems/issues you deal with, and second, the number/quantity/breadth of the issues. Superior capabilities and algorithm helps you deal with the higher complexity of the problem, but it is only higher productivity that will help you deal with the quantity/breadth of issues. At senior levels, the number of people who want your time is far greater than the time you have, the number of things that need your attention is far greater than the number you have handled earlier and the number of simultaneous things you have to manage is far greater than what you have ever done. The breadth is such that one day in the morning, you could be discussing the long-term strategic plan and in the afternoon the same day, you might have to deal with next week's issues. There is an exponential change in the number/quantity/breadth of issues that you have to deal with as you climb up the corporate ladder, and to manage that, you have to drive an exponential increase in your productivity as well.

Again and again, I have seen people move from junior to middle levels and then to senior levels, and fail somewhere on the way. Usually, their failure at the higher levels is mistakenly attributed to a lack of capability. It is not that. Often, it is because they have not grown their productivity in proportion to the higher ask of the senior level. And folks, a productivity increase does not happen by itself, it can't be taken for granted—it has to be catalysed by you.

A classic manifestation of this was a senior person with a fairly independent responsibility. This person was overworked, overwhelmed and trying his level best. Yet, the business was going nowhere, people were unhappy and there were no results to show. This person saw himself or herself as Atlas, carrying the entire load of the business on his or her shoulders, often externalizing to say everything is broken and needs to be fixed, and hence he or she has to work fourteen hours a day and so on. These are classic symptoms of poor productivity—lack of knowing how to be productive in a complex environment, how to organize oneself and manage your energy and time. The Atlas stereotype is a positive mask, but it is a mask—it simply hides the real problem, which is poor productivity. So the next time you are working your butt off but nothing gets done, you know where the problem is. Or the next time you feel that the entire company, your team and your business needs you and you are Atlas and that is the reason you work so hard, you know what the problem is. It is poor productivity.

The 'How' of Productivity

Now that you are aware of the need to catalyse growth in your productivity, let us move on to how to achieve that. Productivity is a complex subject comprising many facets including time management, prioritization, discipline, learning to differentiate the important/urgent from the less important/less urgent, the art of delegation, the skill of multitasking and so on and so forth. Each of these aspects can be a book in itself, and I would encourage all readers to make an effort at getting better at each of them. A good way is through your TMRR process and reflection—identify what you think you need to get better at and then start to focus on that.

In this chapter, however, I am not going to focus on these various facets. Instead, I am going to share some of my experiences of boosting productivity, which catalysts have worked for me and how I have focused on growing my productivity. This is not a replacement for the facets above; these are just my beliefs and learning. I have found two methods that helped catalyse the growth of my productivity. One is derived from Stephen Covey's concept of the 'circle of influence' and the other is my own method of allocating time to my priorities, something I call the 'rocks first' method.

Focus on the Circle of Influence

Two decades ago, I read Stephen Covey's *The Seven Habits of Highly Effective People*, one of the greatest self-development books of the modern era. One of the concepts in the book that I found very interesting was that of the circle of influence. For those of you who have not read the book, I shall briefly explain the concept, focusing on those aspects which are relevant to increasing productivity.

The core of the concept is that broadly, everything that has an effect on you, impacts you and is of consequence to you can be divided into two broad circles. One is called the circle of influence, which comprises all those things that you have an influence on, and the other is the circle of concern, which comprises things that impact you directly or indirectly, but which you can't influence. These are two concentric circles—the inner circle, the smaller circle, which comprises things that you can influence, and the outer circle, the bigger circle, which comprises things on which you don't have an influence. This is schematically represented in the drawing below:

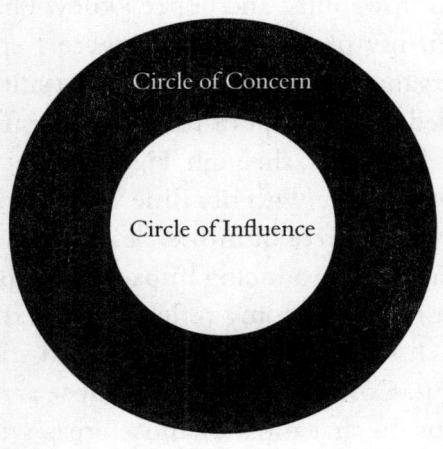

While this concept can be used for all aspects of life, for the purpose of this chapter, I would like you to visualize this in the context of things at work. You dream of being very successful in your career, but to be successful, you must deliver high quality and high quantity of output at work. You must deliver results which are compelling so that people take note of them, and thus create a good reputation and long-term career success for yourself. For you to deliver those results, there are a set of things which are within your sphere of influence, in your circle of influence. Equally, there are things that impact your ability to deliver results at work that are not in your influence, and those are in the outer circle, the circle of concern.

As I became a senior at work, and started facing the productivity problems that all senior managers inevitably face, I felt, 'I am working damn hard, yet I don't seem to be producing results as easily as I did when I was a junior.' I was quite confident that it was not an issue of my ability, and hence I knew I had to find the answer in my productivity, in where I spent time and how I organized myself to produce results. That is when I applied the concept of the circle of influence to productivity. I realized, through TMRR reflection, that I was most productive with my time when I focused on aspects within my circle of influence. In those things, I was like a magician, producing impactful results at will. Equally, I found through my reflection that there were areas on which I spent a lot of my time and still created limited output. Consistent TMRR in those areas led me to the conclusion that most of those areas were in my circle of concern. I realized that spending time on areas in my circle of concern was producing minimal results and was an extraordinary waste of my time, the greatest productivity killer I had.

There, folks, is my simplest, most obvious and yet super effective key to productivity. You are at your productive best when you focus on things which you have an influence on, which you can impact. Avoid spending time on areas where you don't have any influence or impact. The other way of stating the same thing is that 'highly productive people are those who spend *all their time* on things to which they can make a difference, where they have an influence'. Such people are highly productive with their time, and assuming they have good quality experience algorithms, they create fantastic value and results. Such an individual often gets a lot done for one person and can be rather awe-inspiring at times.

Of course, the benefits of this habit go beyond just productivity, as Stephen Covey explains. The more you focus on your circle of influence, the more it grows, and slowly and steadily, it starts to cover more of the areas that earlier fell under your circle of concern. Hence, this habit is also an effective means of growing your influence over time. I would urge readers to read Stephen Covey's book for a clearer understanding. I am limiting my articulation here to the impact this has on personal productivity at work.

Let us further explore what happens when you don't focus on your circle of influence and instead spend time on your circle of concern. Clearly, you don't produce great results and value. Hence it is obvious that the circle of concern is a killer of productivity. But as I reflected on my own experiences, my TMRR told me that the impact was on more than just productivity. I realized that when I spent time in my circle of concern, I felt irritated, angry, frustrated, at times incapable of creating results and inadequate—a whole host of negative emotions. I came to the realization that the circle of concern was not just a productivity killer and a time waster, but it was, more importantly, an energy killer. And the biggest realization for me personally was that it kills energy disproportionate to the time you spend on it. I realized that I might have spent only half an hour on something that was in my circle of concern, but it often destroyed energy and created enough negativity to kill the productivity of a whole day.

This, then, is my second key to productivity—that productivity is not just about productivity of time but also about productivity of energy. I realized that the productivity of energy is destroyed by spending even a small amount of time on the circle of concern, and that energy loss has an impact even when you subsequently start focusing on your circle of influence. Time in the circle of concern is like poison—it takes only a small amount to have a negative impact on the larger whole.

Hence, my two keys to super high productivity, based on my learning in my work life, are:

1. To increase your productivity, focus relentlessly on whatever is in your circle of influence. Spend all your time on what you can make a difference to, even if in the beginning it looks small.
2. Avoid the circle of concern like the plague. It is not about how much time you waste there—maybe you can afford to waste that time—but the more harmful impact of it is the energy it destroys, the negativity it creates in you, which then has a cascading impact even on the time you spend in your circle of influence.

A question that often comes up in my sessions is—'Does that mean I ignore what is in my circle of concern? What if some of that is very important?' I do believe that you must summon the courage to ignore what is in the circle of concern and focus all your time and energy on what is in your circle of influence. That will create a virtuous cycle of productive results, wherein what is in the circle of concern will become less and less important over time. However, for a moment, let us assume there is something in the circle of concern that is so critical that it can't be ignored. Let us say you are a salesperson who has been pursuing a new large deal for a long time. Finally, after many attempts, the customer gives you a trial order and you know that ensuring delivery of that order on time, with no quality defects, is important to create future business. However, this is in the hands of the supply chain team and not fully under your influence. What then is the right way to deal with it?

There are two approaches one can take for what is in your circle of concern.

A truism of life is that everything that is in your circle of concern is in somebody else's circle of influence. In an organization's context, it could mean a co-worker outside your team, a vendor, etc. A good way of dealing with important things in your circle of concern is to identify in whose circle of influence they are, and then strike a partnership with that person. And for any partnership to work, there has to be a win-win situation. This means that there is something in your circle of influence which is of value to that person and you have to create value for him or her in return for your circle of concern issue being addressed. So the first approach is to strike up partnerships.

The second approach to dealing with things in the circle of concern is to find a path to them through your circle of influence. Let's suppose that you are dependent on information and data from a colleague who is not in your team and whom you do not have adequate influence on. In the past, this individual has often given you poor quality information and this has impacted the subsequent work that you do with that data. Now, this is in your circle of concern, and thinking about this creates all the stress and negative energy that circle of concern items create. Are there paths through your circle of influence that lead to a solution? You could possibly call that person and actively teach and coach them how to collect that data and send it to you. In a way, you are doing something which that person's manager should have done. You might think it is a waste of time, but doing this is better than being stressed about your circle of concern. Another possible path through your circle of influence is to give yourself enough time to check the data when it comes and to redo it if required. Both these approaches are within your circle of influence, stuff you can do. But what most people do is spend a lot of time agonizing about something in their circle of concern, in the process creating negativity and destroying productivity, instead of finding simple pathways through their circle of influence to issues in their circle of concern. In chapter 7, we will apply this approach of finding pathways through the circle of influence to the more complex problem of how to find a good boss, an issue that is in everybody's circle of concern.

The 'Rocks First' Method

Apart from the circle of influence approach, the other method I have personally used to keep my productivity high is the 'rocks first' method. Before I talk about it, I would like to narrate a story that I am sure each one of you has come across at some time or the other. A teacher takes a glass jar and places it on the table along with some sand and rocks. In the first instance, she pours all the sand into the jar, which becomes nearly full, and thereafter can accommodate only a couple of rocks. In the second instance, she puts all the rocks into the jar and then pours the sand on top of that. The sand flows into the spaces between the rocks. A fair amount of sand is in the jar, only some is left. So in the first instance, all the sand is consumed but very few rocks; in the second instance, all the rocks and a good quantity of the sand are consumed. The trick lay in putting the rocks in first. The teacher then goes on to tell the class that the rocks are the more important things in your life—your health, your relationships, your learning, etc. The sand is the less important or trivial things. If you come to the rocks after dealing with the sand, you will only deal with a few important things; the bulk of the important things will not be dealt with. However, if you turn it around and first deal with the rocks, the important things, then you will get a lot done and will have to deal with only as much sand as you have space for.

This is what I see on a daily basis in workplaces around me—people spending all their time on sand and getting very few rocks into the jar. Most people feel that they know their priorities, they know what is important. However, they mistakenly assume that just because they know what is important, they are actually prioritizing it and dealing with it. That is a myth. It is more likely that you know what is important, what your rocks are, but the bulk of your time and energy is still spent on the sand.

To make sure people understand, I often do an exercise with them. On one sheet of paper, I make them write what they think is important, things which, if they did them well, would create learning, lead to career success and make them feel productive. Once they have written this on a sheet of paper, we fold it away, not to be opened till later. Then I ask them what all they did the previous month—which activities they did, where they spent their time, energy and money/resources and where they got their teams to spend their time/money/ resources. It's a detailed exercise. After that, based on where they spent their time/energy/resources, we try and write down which of these could have been important. If time/energy/resources were spent on them, then these would have been considered important, so in a way, we retrospectively derive what would have been important. This list of 'derived important' things is then written on another sheet of paper.

Then comes the most interesting part. We compare the two sheets of paper—the first sheet, what people thought was important to them, and the second list, the derived important things. I am sure you are not surprised when I say that in most cases, there is very little in common between the two lists. This is the greatest tragedy of productivity—that most people do not actually spend their time/energy/resources on what they think is important to them. This is true of life in general, but let us focus here on work. At work, people know what is important, they know that focusing on the important things will produce results, get them success, create value and learning and sharpen their algorithms. The tragedy is that despite knowing that, most people do not spend their time/energy/resources at work on those things, and hence never achieve the success they are capable of.

In my own professional journey, I know I was blessed to have an in-built God-given TMRR model, which kept sharpening my algorithm. It is my privilege and my blessing to have been born with that. But despite that, for a fair share of my career, I knew I was not producing the kind of impact I could, the kind of value I was capable of. And then one day, the bolt from my TMRR struck. I reflected and realized the reason for it—it was the sand and rocks disease. I knew what the important things were, but I did not have a process to ensure that I spent my time/energy/resources on these things. My time was being consumed by the sand first. That is when I came up with the second approach I have been following to manage my productivity, the method of allocating time to the 'rocks first'.

It is a very simple approach I have been following for many years now. At the beginning of each month, I make a list of important things, things I consider priorities. I force myself to order this as well, putting the most important ones at the top. Most times, this list is not very different from the list of the previous month, and that is how it should be; priorities should not change often. But I do make this list each month. Then I start by allocating time in my calendar for the next month, starting with the most important things at the top. Once I have given as much time as the top item requires, I move to the next item, and so on. I keep moving down my priority list till I have allocated 85 per cent of the time I have for the next month. The balance 15 per cent is what I leave for the unavoidable sand that all of us have to deal with. This

85 per cent is formalized, it is in my calendar, and I have developed the discipline to never compromise on this. I never allow the sand to replace one of the rocks. This approach of a formal 'calendared' allocation of time at work, to what I consider the rocks, has been among the greatest productivity unlocks of my work life.

This also had some interesting unintended benefits. It significantly improved my delegation. It became very simple for me—if it was not one of the rocks I had time for, if it was not in my calendar with allocated time, then I didn't need to do it myself. Every such thing is delegable and one of my team members can do it. I delegated a great deal and ensured that I got out of the way of my team in such things. 'You decide, you do it, it is not in my calendar, it is not a rock for me' was my mantra. And that delegation freed me and at the same time energized my team. They had a set of things they could do with complete freedom, without worrying that the boss was constantly breathing down their necks.

My assertion to each one of you is that too much of your time is being spent managing the sand. It is a myth to assume that because you know what the rocks are, you are spending your time, energy and money on these. It does not happen by itself; you need to catalyse the process of ensuring that you are actually focusing on the rocks. I told you what my method is. It is simple, and you can follow it as well. Equally, you can find your own method. Either way, make sure that you are catalysing the attention to the rocks. Left to itself, it is always the sand that flows into the jar first.

So these are my two methods to higher productivity—the circle of influence approach and the 'rocks first' approach. Despite these approaches, I wouldn't say I am at my productive best all the time; it is a very difficult thing to be. But again, thanks to my TMRR, I have figured out how to recognize when I am not at my productive best. I have learnt that the symptom to look out for is the feeling of frustration. Frustration happens when you feel you are doing your best and yet things are not moving ahead. Then I go back and analyse why. I assess whether the circle of concern is taking up too much of my focus. I go back and check whether I am spending my time/energy/resources on the rocks. Typically, the problem would be in one of these areas, and once I correct it, I can sense my productivity come back up fairly quickly. I would urge each one of you also to try and recognize the symptoms for yourself when you are in a low productivity phase. Recognize the symptoms and fix the problem soon. I would be willing to place a wager that whenever you feel frustrated, if you stop and analyse why, there is a very high probability that you are in your circle of concern. Time and energy that is gone can never come back. Be at your productive best for as much of your work life as possible as it is crucial for your success.

Unleash the Catalyst

1. To be successful, to generate real individual growth, just developing your experience algorithm is not enough. You have to employ that algorithm in a

highly productive way. Your productivity is the means by which you convert your experience algorithm into value and results for yourself and your organization.

2. The higher you go in the corporate ladder, the more the need to grow your productivity. And your productivity does not increase by itself; it has to be catalysed to grow.

3. The catalysts I have used in my work life for my productivity are:

   a. Relentless focus on the circle of influence and avoiding like a plague what is in the circle of concern.

   b. Having a disciplined 'rocks first' time-allocation system, where I ensure that I provide my time/energy for the rocks and not the sand.

4. If you'd like to, you can use my methods. If not, you can develop your own. Whatever be the method, please do not ignore your productivity.

Unleashing the Catalyst: Summarizing Part I and Setting Up Part II

In Part I, we have covered the means to driving real individual growth in three important concepts:

1. Converting time into experience is the very bedrock of real individual growth. An effective TMRR model is the key to converting the time you are spending at work into an experience algorithm that will drive your success in the future.
2. Applying the TMRR algorithm on major learning cycles is an exponential way to drive real individual growth.
3. Just building the experience algorithm is not enough. You have to parallelly grow your productivity. Productivity is the means through which you can convert the experience algorithm into results. The key to growing productivity is to focus on the circle of influence and to make sure you allocate your time to the rocks and not the sand.

However, real individual growth has to be backed by good career management. I have often seen individuals with fantastic experience algorithms and productivity being tripped up by poor career decisions which they then struggle to recover from. We are very much in a VUCA (volatility, uncertainty, complexity and ambiguity) world, including in how careers develop and how they are managed. It is important to have the right approach to managing your career, to make the right career decisions, if you want to convert your real individual growth into long-term career success. And the beauty is, the principle remains the same—focus on the deeds and the results will come. Focus on real individual growth, which is the driver of career success, and that career success will be yours.

The next section, Part II, is about career management. It is about helping you understand how to make career decisions while focusing on real individual growth.

PART II

5

Win Where It Matters

Most of us have heard the story of the hare and the tortoise. It is the story of the race between the swift, agile rabbit and the slow, lumbering tortoise. The rabbit starts at a rapid pace and then takes a break, while the lumbering tortoise carries on without a break and finally wins the race. The moral of the story is that slow and steady wins the race. When I see youngsters today chasing careers, it often looks like the story of the rabbit. They get out of the blocks in a hurry, want a frenetic pace of career growth in the initial stages and then lose steam where it matters, near the finish line. I do not advocate 'slow and steady wins the race' for careers. But I do have an adaptation of that moral for professional success and that is—win where it matters. You don't have to win all the time. If you want to have a truly glorious career, then it is important that you win in the second half of your career. That's the only thing that matters; everything else is immaterial. That is my career moral: win where it matters—in the second half of your career.

Careers today are roughly around forty years long, and it is important to internalize that it is a marathon, not a sprint. A person's career can broadly be split into two halves, the first half and the second half. The length of the two halves is not important and does not have to be mathematically equal—it can be twenty years each, it can be twenty-five and fifteen or eighteen and twenty-two. The broad concept is that careers have two halves.

I have observed many people through the journey of their careers. I have seen those who succeeded, those who were less successful, those who looked like they had a good start but did not achieve their potential, those who looked like they had a bad start but seemed to overachieve, those whose careers had twists and turns and those whose careers had more steady, straight paths. Having observed all these people and their careers—and it is a lifetime of observation—I have come to two conclusions:

1. The more significant career achievements are often in the second half of the career.
2. Most people succeed in the first halves of their careers, very few in the second.

The Second Half Is Where True Success Is Created

Let us start with the first conclusion: The more significant career achievements are often in the second half of the career. A good way of understanding this is to compare two people with similar qualifications and capabilities who passed out of the same college at the same time. Let us say we compare their careers after forty years, when they hang up their boots, and conclude that one of them had a very successful career with great accomplishments and the second had a more moderate career with fewer accomplishments. Let us say the first person had a career of 100 points and the second person had a career of sixty points, and the gap in their career success was forty points. The interesting thing you will find is that the first half of the career often explains only a very small portion of the success difference, say only five of the forty points, while the bulk of the success difference—thirty-five points—is explained by the difference in their success in the second half.

If you continue to do this comparison for various professions, you will find the same story playing out. Let us compare two people with a marketing major from the same business school. You will find that both were possibly heads of marketing for decent-sized businesses at the end of the first halves of their careers, but at the end of the second halves, one of them went on to become a global CMO of a big MNC while the other did not make more progress than what he or she had achieved at the end of the first half. If you look at two engineers who passed out at the same time, you will find that both of them went on to possibly head large plants as a plant manager at the end of the first halves of their careers, but one of them went on to then become the head of a company's end-to-end supply chain and manufacturing while the other continued to stay as plant manager or do functional jobs. One could do this again and again and in most cases you will reach the same conclusion—most people of similar qualifications and capabilities achieve roughly the same career success and results in the first halves of their careers, but there is an extraordinary difference of success in the second halves. This then led me to the conclusion that the more significant career achievements are often in the second half of the career.

Career Success—Easy in the First Half, Difficult in the Second Half

As I observed the careers of several people, I saw that most seemed to have achieved something in the first halves of their careers. Differences in capabilities and potential did not seem to have created a stark difference in the first halves of careers. Equally, I found that most people find it difficult to succeed in the second halves. It is almost like you keep progressing steadily, growing in your career in the first half, and then that growth suddenly slows down and almost comes to a stop in the second half. As a thumb rule, I would say 95 per cent of people are successful in the first halves of their careers, but it is the other way round in the second halves where only 5 per cent succeed and 95 per cent fail. 'Fail' is a provocative word, I admit, but what I really mean is that 95 per cent don't really make much progress in their careers in the second halves beyond what they have already achieved in the first.

The question that naturally follows is the 'why' of it—why do most people find it easy to succeed in the first halves of their careers and difficult to succeed in the second? There are three factors that explain this:

1. The nature of the organizational pyramid.
2. The impact of the boss and supervisors.
3. The preparation required to succeed at each level.

The Nature of the Organizational Pyramid

The nature of the organizational pyramid in the first half of a person's career differs from the second half. In the early phase of their careers, people are at the bottom of the pyramid, which has a wider base, while in the later stage of their careers, they are in the narrower part of the organizational pyramid. In the first half, the wider base of the organizational pyramid creates more opportunities. The operating principle is that if you are good enough to do the job at the next level, then opportunity is not a constraint. There are enough opportunities at that level. Hence, career progress in the first half is a function of the absolute, not the relative. If you are good enough, then by virtue of the pyramid, you will move ahead. However, in the second half, the organizational pyramid is narrower. Fewer opportunities come up. Also, every time an opportunity comes up, there are many more claimants. Hence, moving up is not just a function of how good you are, but also of how good you are relative to others. Another factor is that if an opportunity comes around and you don't get it, then the person who gets it stays in that role for 4–5 years. Tenures at the senior levels are longer, and so the next opportunity often does not come immediately. To summarize, there are fewer opportunities in the second half and those few opportunities are determined on relativity and not absolute capability. Hence, opportunity becomes a constraint in the second half of your career.

Impact of the Boss

The second factor is the impact of the boss and of supervision, which is much higher in the first half than in the second. In the first half, the results we produce are not just a function of our capabilities and what we do, but also a function of the very active supervision we get from our bosses and the hierarchy of our organization. In the first half, bosses and the organizational systems and processes make up for weaknesses that individuals have, and hence, it does not impede their career progress. However, in the second half, the supervision that people receive from their bosses and others in the organization is limited. Results have to be produced based on your own capabilities, and impact can be measured far more accurately. There is nobody to compensate for weaknesses, which are often exposed at this stage, and so people 'fail' more often in the second halves of their careers.

Preparation for the Next Level

The third factor is the preparation required to succeed at the next level. In the first halves of careers, the next, higher role is somewhat similar to the current role, and so the current role often allows a degree of preparation for the next. E.g. somebody could go from being an assistant brand manager to a brand manager or from an area sales manager to a regional sales manager for a larger geography. In each of these examples, the current level offered the opportunity for a degree of preparation, as the next level is simply a more complex, higher-scale version of the current job. However, in the second halves of careers at senior levels, the next job is often fundamentally different from the previous one. It could be a transition from being head of sales to being a CEO, which is the transition from being a functional expert to a business leader. It could be a transition from being a plant head to being the head of the end-to-end supply chain, a transition from technical skills to a more strategic and holistic responsibility. In each of these, the current job of the individual does not prepare them adequately to succeed at the next level, and so people often have to learn after getting there in order to succeed. This is another key reason why people experience more success in the first halves and more failure in the second halves of their careers.

To reiterate, the three factors that explain why most people succeed in the first halves of their careers, and very few in the second, as explained above are: the nature of the organizational pyramid, the impact of the boss and supervisors and, lastly, the preparation required to succeed at each level.

So let's look at the two conclusions that we have arrived at:

1. The more significant career achievements are often in the second half of the career.
2. Most people succeed in the first halves of their careers, very few in the second.

The two together set up the career challenge for most people: *where you need to succeed is where it is more difficult to succeed*. The second half is where you need to succeed and yet that is when it is more difficult to succeed. And hence you need a catalyst, the catalyst of foundation-building in the first half, to ensure success in the second half.

While the success that matters is success in the second half, the foundation of that success is often laid entirely in the first half. Far too often, people get to the second halves of their careers, recognize that they do not have the necessary skills and capabilities to succeed there and come to the painful realization that it is too late to pick up these skills and capabilities. They have not invested in the right foundation in the first halves, on which the pillars of success in the second halves are built. The most visible symptom of this is the spectre of people past the age of fifty nearing the end of their careers who often stagnate and are not able to contribute meaningfully. Mostly, these people also realize that they fail to keep up and contribute, but despite trying hard, they fail to acquire the skills at that age to make a difference. This is visible in most organizations, especially in more humane organizations which let such people serve out their tenure and retire gracefully. Youngsters in these organizations often look at these people and snigger among themselves. In private conversations, they are often referred to as the 'old guard' or 'passengers'. What is interesting is that these youngsters are usually not thinking of how they can build their foundations in the first halves to avoid the same trap of turning into the 'old guard' of tomorrow.

What Are You Managing Your First Half for?

Success in the second halves of people's careers is largely a function of the foundation and pillars built in the first halves. This means that every person, in the first half of his or her career, must be focused not only on winning then and there, but must have a very sharp focus on building the foundation for succeeding when it matters. I want you to pause for a minute and answer this question: 'Am I managing my first half to succeed in the first half, or am I managing my first half to succeed in the second?' Reflect on this question for a while and get a clear answer for yourself.

The ideal answer to this question is obvious. As explained earlier, most people succeed in the first halves of their careers, and so there is little more to be gained by focusing all your efforts in the first half for immediate success. Equally, we have concluded, the greater career achievements are often in the second half, and very few succeed in the second. Based on this, one would think it would be obvious that most people would spend some of their focus in the first halves on preparing to succeed in the second. Unfortunately, in my experience, this does not happen. Most people I observe are so busy chasing their tails that they hardly build the foundation required to succeed when it matters. They don't focus on building the foundation in the first half, which is the catalyst for success in the second half.

The question then is, if it is so obvious that there is tremendous ROI in focusing on foundation-building in the first half rather than chasing short-term career success, then why is it not practised? I believe there are three reasons for this: inability to delay gratification, being in the rat race of comparing self with others and, lastly, lack of knowledge and guidance in building the foundation.

Delaying Gratification

Focusing on foundation-building in the first half does require the mindset of foundation-building and, sometimes, the ability to delay gratification. Let me make a couple of analogies to explain this.

Let's take a junior artist who is apprenticing under a senior artist. In art, all the kudos always goes to the senior artist, who is the face of the art form. The junior spends a few years with the senior and learns key skills on a rapid basis. But there is a gnawing thought in the back of the mind—'When will I get recognized as a great artist?' All the recognition goes to the senior artist, even if the art has been created jointly. To get recognition, however, the junior artist has to break free and do his or her own work. That would bring recognition, but that is the end of the learning in the apprenticeship. If a junior artist breaks free too early because he is not able to manage the thought of not being recognized, then he might get some early recognition, but he wouldn't have built the foundation for a successful career in art for fifty years. This is about the mindset of delaying gratification—the mindset that says that I can live without recognition for a few more years, but by being an apprentice I will invest in my foundation-building during this period so that I am successful in the longer term.

Another analogy is the literal analogy of foundation-building for a tower or a monument. The more complex, taller and more imposing the building you want to make, the more the time required in preparing the drawings, planning the construction and then laying the foundation under the ground. Often, for a complex building, over half the time could be spent planning, preparing drawings and in the foundation-building process. Till that is done, there is nothing tangible to show. If somebody does not have the patience for foundation-building, and they short-circuit the process, they might put up a tall building, but in all probability, it will crash soon. Constructing a tall building requires that you spend enough time planning, drawing and building the foundation.

Careers are like that—to build a tall career, enough time has to be spent preparing, planning, apprenticing and building the foundation. The science of that and the logic of that are often intuitively understood by most people. However, despite that understanding, many people don't do it because they don't have the mindset that can delay gratification in the preparation and foundation-building phase. The lack of this mindset is why, despite it being so obvious, most people do not spend time in the first half building for the second half. Instead, they mistakenly focus on success in the first half.

The Pressure to Be the Best 'Rat' in the Race

The second reason why people do not focus on foundation-building in the first half is the constant need to be in the rat race and win it. Unfortunately, in most cases, the markers we set for how well we are doing in the first half are not defined by how we are learning, what experience we are building, which skills we are acquiring or how we are setting ourselves up for sustainable success through foundation-building. Instead, they are defined by how we are doing in the rat race, how our career is looking versus our peers', how many promotions we have had versus another person who is of a similar profile, etc. This need for constant comparison with others and for winning the short-term rat race is often the primary reason they make poor choices in the first halves of their careers—choices which make them think they are winning the race then and there, but which are not good for foundation-building and hence actually reduce their ability to win the race where it matters—the second half.

Lack of Knowledge and Guidance

The third reason for people to not focus on foundation-building in the first half is actually the lack of knowledge and guidance on how to do so. There is very little quality guidance, mentorship and tabulated knowledge on how to manage one's career in the first half for success in the second half. How does one make the right choices? What does foundation-building mean? Which skills and knowledge are relevant? What is the right balance between width and depth? There are many such questions. Often, the key question in people's mind is, if I am letting go of something that looks lucrative here and now, then how do I know what I am doing instead is indeed building my foundation? Sometimes, people do rely on their seniors within the companies they work for such guidance, but the challenge in these situations is often the impartiality of the guidance. Is the guidance impartial, or is it motivated by the interests of the organization and the seniors? And even if the advice is impartial, is the recipient willing to believe that? Let us suppose there is a finance manager who has spent time learning supply chain finance and the sales side of finance for ten years in a large company. One day, out of the blue, a small company wants that person to be the CFO. It is possible that people within the company advise that person of the need to still learn treasury and accounting, and that the learning is incomplete. However, the challenge for the person is to be able to distinguish between genuine advice and an effort by the organization to prevent that person from leaving. It is indeed very difficult to know that, to know if it is genuine or not. Only when individuals have enough knowledge of the principles of foundation-building will they have the ability to process that advice and select the right one.

In summary, there is a fundamental knowledge lacuna in what it takes to build the foundation to succeed in the second half. A major focus of this book in the succeeding chapters is to fill this knowledge gap. However, the mindset to delay gratification and the ability to not be in the rat race all the time are aspects you will have to build into your personalities and into your behaviours. These aspects are as important for success as the knowledge you will gain from this book.

Unleash the Catalyst

1. To truly succeed in your career, you need to win when it matters, which is the second half. Most people win in the first half, very few in the second.
2. However, success in the second half does not happen based on what you do in the second half. It has to be catalysed by the foundation-building you do in the first.

3. Foundation-building in the first half is easier said than done. There are three key barriers people have to overcome to do the foundation-building:

   a. Inability to delay gratification.
   b. The pressure of winning the rat race.
   c. Lack of knowledge and suitable guidance on how to do foundation-building.

The next few chapters will focus on the knowledge of foundation-building. However, the inability to delay gratification and the temptation to be in the rat race are barriers that you have to overcome yourself.

6

First Half Is the Catalyst Half

A young manager, with about five years of experience, once came to me for advice. A year ago, he had moved to a factory after four years at the corporate office. Within a year of moving to the factory, he heard that his earlier boss in the corporate office was leaving, and the company wanted him to come back and take up that role. He was not sure what to do. He had spent just one year at the factory, but the more senior corporate role that was being offered to him ahead of time was tempting. Should he stay in the factory and complete his foundation-building there or should he take the more senior corporate role, which provided a promotion and more senior management exposure?

This is the kind of question people often face in their careers in the first halves. The challenge they face is that there are no clear principles laid out on how to take such decisions. And in the absence of such principles, people most often choose higher promotions, higher pay and whatever makes them feel more successful in their careers then and there. In the previous chapter, we established the need for focusing on foundation-building in the first half, which becomes the catalyst for success in the second half. The question is, what are the principles of foundation-building, and how can one help people make career decisions keeping the catalyst of foundation-building in mind?

There are a set of three career management principles which, if you adopt in your first half, can easily catalyse foundation-building for the second half. These three principles that I strongly advocate are: focus on depth over width, complete major learning cycles and get out there when you can.

Depth over Width

The first career management principle for foundation-building is 'depth over width'. In my judgement, depth in a few things in the first half of your career is much better for building the foundation than width in many things. I say that because depth builds skills, while width primarily builds knowledge and information. I believe that in the era we are in, it is primarily skills and capabilities that determine long-term success. Knowledge has become universal and accessible and is no longer the driver of long-term success.

Let me give you an example of what I mean. A lot of people in the early stages of their careers get to do front-line jobs. Let's assume there are two people, Amit and

Vijay, who spend three years in front-line sales. Amit spends the three years in the same city managing the same product lines and accounts while Vijay spends the three years in three different cities, one year in each. Vijay gains a lot of knowledge and information. He finds out how the market is different in different cities, how the product lines that sell in each city are different and how the retailers of each city behave somewhat differently from those in other cities. He picks up a much higher width of information and knowledge. Amit, on the other hand, acquires the knowledge of only one city, and hence has less width of information and knowledge compared to Vijay. However, Amit, by virtue of having spent three years in depth in the same city, builds better skills and capabilities. E.g. Amit, in the second and third year, will be able to assess and learn from the impact of what he did in the first year. He will be able to see what worked well and what did not in subsequent years. That understanding allows him to build the experience algorithm, and if he can use TMRR in a disciplined way, then the algorithm-building is even stronger. Compare that to Vijay, who, because he is not in the same city the next year, cannot assess the impact of what he did in the previous year and hence cannot build the same quality of algorithm. What happens when these two people get to the second halves of their careers? Vijay, who spent time in three different cities, gets to the second half with a lot of information and knowledge, but not a strong experience algorithm, while Amit gets to the second half with less knowledge and information, but with a stronger algorithm. And what drives success in the second half is the quality of the algorithm you come with. Knowledge is easily available, information can easily be found in this Internet era, and it is not a prerequisite for success in the second half. In fact, too much knowledge can be a barrier at times, as knowledge and information is continuously changing, and if you are a prisoner of past knowledge, then you are not able to accept new knowledge and information easily. What you would rather have in your second half is the foundational skills and the experience algorithm that gives you the ability to analyse and deal with any knowledge pool that you have to face.

The other difference that develops between Amit and Vijay is the skill of capturing high-hanging fruit. I have always believed that the first year of any job you do is the easiest year for two reasons. One, there are typically low expectations in the first year, and hence it is easier to meet them. The other reason is that in the first year, one can have success by finding low-hanging fruit. In any situation in a new job, it is relatively easy to find something that is not working well or something that is an obvious thing to do, basically low-hanging fruit, and focusing on that makes you successful. However, if you do the same job for three years, it becomes difficult to find low-hanging fruit in the second and third years, which means perforce one has to become skilled and experienced at finding high-hanging fruit and in plucking it, solving problems for it and creating value. Now imagine a person who, in the first half of his or her career, has done many jobs, each for brief periods, and so has primarily learnt only to find and solve for low-hanging fruit. When such a person gets to the second half, where success does not come easy, where, to be successful, you have to be able to find high-hanging fruit and solve problems for it, they are not able to do it. They have never built the skill required for that, a classic case of not building the foundation in the first half for success in the second half.

So it is very important, in your first half, to focus on depth in career management. Manage your career so that you get relatively long periods in roles and you acquire significant depth in some functional areas—which enables skill and algorithm-building—for these are the foundations you need to build to catalyse success in the second half of your career. Equally, do not fall into the trap of chasing width in the first half of your career. The need to be in the rat race, the need to feel continuously successful, can often push you to making career decisions where you experience a lot of width, many jobs, many companies, many cities and many functions. This will build a lot of knowledge, but unfortunately, this is unlikely to be effective in the foundational skill and algorithm-building that you require. Such people feel hyper-successful in the first half, they feel they are ahead in the rat race, and then get to the second half and get a shock. They have simply not built the algorithm and skills to succeed there, and the rat race comes to a stop.

Complete Major Learning Cycles

The second principle of career management in the first half deals with how you manage learning cycles. There are two key things to manage to ensure that your career benefits from learning cycles.

1. Are you taking career decisions in your first half in a way that results in you experiencing full, end-to-end learning cycles, as opposed to experiencing many half and incomplete ones?
2. Are your career decisions maximizing the opportunity to participate in major learning cycles and to fully juice the ones you participate in?

Starting with the first, in my judgement, the experience algorithmic benefit of full learning cycles is many times higher than that of many half cycles. Going through two half learning cycles is not equal to one full learning cycle. E.g. let's say in a new product learning cycle, you learn how to spot the opportunity and develop the brief, do product development and testing, and then you change roles or jobs. Then with another new product, you learn how to build a launch strategy, launch in the market, ask for feedback and take corrective action. On paper, you have experienced the full product learning cycle, but in two halves. Experiencing a learning cycle in two halves is significantly less effective than experiencing a full learning cycle end-to-end in one go. The reason for this is in how it aids algorithm-building. If you participate in two half learning cycles, you might learn all the activities concerning that process and initiative, but you do not get to understand how the decisions you made in the first half of the learning cycle worked out. You do not get the opportunity to apply TMRR in a holistic way, and hence you significantly reduce the algorithm-building. If you find that your career decisions are repeatedly making you experience several incomplete learning cycles, then you are risking failure in the second half of your career.

Having established that, it would be impossible in your career to complete every single learning cycle you have the opportunity to be a part of. You would have to leave midway as you change roles or move along in your career. So while the preferred situation is to achieve the completion of all learning cycles, the question is, if you do have to exit midway, then what is the key guideline? My advice is to never walk out of a major learning cycle in your career. Overall, you will experience many cycles in a long career. However, among all those cycles, there would be only a few major learning cycles. Major learning cycles are those which are career-defining, those that have the greatest impact on building your algorithm. I feel most people get the opportunity for about 4–5 major learning cycles in their entire career of about forty years. These few major learning cycles are often what determine a person's future success. One of the great skills of career management is to recognize when you are in a major learning cycle, and then to be sure that you do not make a career choice that hampers the completion of the said learning cycle. Sometimes, in the first half of your career, you might be tempted by a promotion or a new job when you are slap bang in the middle of a major learning cycle. These are the toughest career decisions to make. My advice remains—when in the first half of your career, always favour what drives real individual growth, always favour completing the major learning cycle.

Sometimes people say to me, 'I am in a major learning cycle and I want to complete it, but my organization wants me to do a new job that will result in me leaving it incomplete.' This might happen to you too. Even when you find yourself in such a situation, I am of the view that you must try to complete the major learning cycle if you are in one. Here is how I think about this situation: if you are in a major learning cycle, it also, in all probability, means that you are doing something very important and critical for the business. It is highly unlikely that you are in a major learning cycle doing something that is unimportant to the business. Hence, it should be possible to have conversations with your managers and leaders in which you tell them that you want to complete the learning cycle and in the process also want to make sure that you complete the critical initiative for the company. Most companies are reasonable, they will actually appreciate somebody having such a viewpoint, and I am sure they will more than make up in the future for the opportunity that you let go now. So when you are in a major learning cycle, try your best to complete it. There are very few major learning cycle opportunities and they are too precious to be missed.

In a career spanning twenty-five years, while I have experienced many learning cycles, there have only been four major learning cycles. I want to describe some of them for the benefit of the readers. It was in my first

company, Asian Paints, that I experienced two major
learning cycles in about a decade. The first was early
on, when I was a brand/product manager. It was a cycle
in which I spent over three years at a go, learning the
fundamentals of marketing, something that has stood me
in good stead all my life. Most people at an early career
stage like that do not spend three years in one role. I did,
and it was a major learning cycle for me. I resisted the
temptation to keep seeking change, and I had a mentor
who helped me make the right choices at that stage.
The second major learning cycle for me was when I was
fortunate to be made part of an end-to-end organization
transformation project, working along with a consulting
company. The project lasted six months, possibly the
most enlightening six months of my career, but the
learning cycle lasted over three years. During these three
years, many of the recommendations from the project
stage were implemented, and I could continuously add
to my algorithm by understanding what we did in the
project stage was working and what was not. In hindsight,
I think I made a poor career choice after those three years
as I was still in a super zone of learning, but was tempted
by a bigger salary and title from another company. I feel
that if I had done one more year in that learning cycle, I
would have built an even better experience algorithm for
myself. I probably got only 75 per cent of the value from
that cycle. The next learning cycle was when I joined a
new company in a turnaround situation. The business
was not performing well when I joined, and there were
many days when I felt it was a hopeless situation and

that it was taking too much effort for no return. Yet, with some persistence, I stayed there for four years, effected a successful turnaround and, in the process, experienced one of my major learning cycles. It taught me how to turn around an underperforming business, how to deal with adversity and how to motivate people in difficult situations. My next major learning cycle was when I made a cross-functional move from being a business leader all my life to being the HR head for Cadbury India. This cycle involved learning an entirely new space and then creating value. I did it for three years and saw the value being created, understood which of my business skills mattered in HR and, most importantly, gave myself enough time so that the theoretical aspects of HR actually penetrated the practical aspects of my leadership style and changed me as a leader. The greatest impact of a major learning cycle is when it changes you as a human being, and I gave myself enough time and opportunity in that learning cycle to see myself change.

Get out There When You Can

The third principle for me is getting out there when you can. One of the key foundational elements of career management is building business understanding from the trenches, not from the ivory towers. It is vital in the first half to spend enough time in the trenches. This could be in front-line sales facing customers, in factories or in highly transaction-intensive operational roles. This could mean spending time in challenging locations that are not idyllic to live in. Much like how you can't become an effective general leading an army if you don't have an understanding of what happens in the trenches, you can't become an effective senior leader if you don't understand the nuts and bolts of how business happens. The critical thing is to try and do as much of this as you can in the first half of your career, preferably the first quarter of your career. That's because there are more operational nuts-and-bolts roles available at that stage. It is difficult to get to twenty years' experience, realize that you have not done your time in the trenches and then find a role suitable for doing that at that level of seniority. Equally, life stage and personal preferences also play a role; early in their careers, people have greater flexibility to choose locations that might be more challenging to live in, roles that are more operational and time-intensive, than at a later life stage, where other priorities might come in. Success in the second half is often a function of being able to understand and relate to what is happening in the bowels of the business, the challenges in the trenches and how the strategy that you are developing will actually work where it matters—out there. If you have not been out there in the foundational stage of your career, then you are not going to be able to leverage this understanding when you need it in the second half. When you look back at your first half, you must be able to see that some of the time you spent there was like annealing steel in a furnace— challenging and intense. If it has been a comfortable ride all the time, it is possibly an indicator that you have not got out there yet.

A personal annealing, 'out there' experience for me was right after my MBA, during my first year at Asian Paints. I was out there in Jaipur as a trainee. Right in the first month, the godown keeper had an exigency and the godown was unmanned. Since the crucial festival season was ahead, I was asked to manage the godown for the next few months. Here I was, an MBA from a premier business school counting boxes in a godown, making sure it matched what was in the invoices and everything that had to be dispatched for the day was sent out before I went home. One might ask, was there any foundation-building experience in counting boxes? I can assure you there was. I figured out in those four months that a lot of people who design boxes have probably not spent enough time counting boxes in godowns. The markings on the boxes often made it challenging to pick the right ones, and the batch numbers and dates did not make FIFO easy. Some products never sold in full boxes, which meant that every box had to be opened, which meant the count of items in each box was not planned well. I could go on and on, but to put it simply, in the many years that followed and the many boxes I designed in my career, I always kept that godown in mind. I knew what it took to work in the godown—the trenches, so to say.

So these, then, are my three principles for foundation-building in the first half—favour depth over width, complete major learning cycles and get out there when you can. The basis of these principles comes down to being clear that the objective of career management in the first half is foundation-building for the second half, as opposed to success in the first half.

One way of checking if you are making foundation-building decisions is to ask this question: how would your career decisions in the first half be different if the objective was success in the first half, instead of foundation-building for the second half? In many cases, the career decisions required for success in the first half and foundation-building for the second half might coincide. These are the easy decisions to make. The challenge is when you come across a situation—the kind I described at the beginning of this chapter where a young manager had to choose between continuing in the factory and taking the promotion at the corporate office—where the career decision you have to make to maximize success in the first half is at odds with what will be good for foundation-building for the second half. My exhortation to you, dear readers, is please prioritize foundation-building for the second half. Don't get tempted by low-hanging fruit, by the allure of looking successful early in your career. It will not really be important by the time you hang up your boots. Make decisions based on what will lead to real individual growth, what will improve your experience algorithm and what will drive foundation-building. When in doubt, adhere to the principles—favour depth over width, complete major learning cycles when you are in them and get out there when you can.

Unleash the Catalyst

1. Foundation-building in the first half is the catalyst for success in the second half. To make the right career

choices in the first half, take decisions that maximize real individual growth rather than short-term career success.

2. Focusing on career choices that favour depth over width is important for foundation-building. Depth drives skill-building, which is more important for the experience algorithm in the longer term. Length in roles also allows you to learn how to get to high-hanging fruit, which is important for success in the second half.

3. There will be many learning cycles that you will experience in your career. However, out of these many, there would be only 4–5 major learning cycles. These will be the career-defining ones. It is important to know when you are in one of them. Always take decisions that allow you to complete a major learning cycle; never leave one incomplete.

4. Get out there when you can. It is important to learn the nuts and bolts of business early in your career.

7

Bosses and Mentors as Catalysts

As I observed and analysed the careers of successful people and less successful people, one thing became amply clear to me—success was not just a function of what each person did, there was a significant impact that others had on the success of people. And often, the most important 'other' person was the boss they had in their foundational work years (say the first fifteen years of their work life). In this era of alpha people, who believe they can do anything and everything by themselves, it was interesting to observe that actually, a lot of success that people experience in their careers is not just because of what they did, but also, in great measure, because of the quality of bosses they had in their foundational years. The more I observed people, the clearer it became that there is a catalysing impact that your bosses in your foundational years have on your long-term career success. This is an inescapable truth. It is very easy to succeed in your long-term career if you have had great bosses in your foundational years. Equally, the odds of long-term career success are significantly diminished if you have had poor bosses in your foundational years. In a way, what I am saying is that your career success is not just a function of what you do, but is also greatly impacted by others. A thought that is difficult to accept, but as I said, it's an inescapable truth.

Let us first try to understand the 'why' of it. Why do bosses in foundational years make such a difference to your long-term career success? From what I have seen of bosses and managers, there are broadly two kinds. The first type of boss is one who is focused on getting results out of his or her subordinates. Their primary orientation is to get the job done, and so they follow up, support and drive you to get results. The second type of boss is one who is equally committed to delivering results, but does that so that you not only deliver results but also learn and build your experience algorithm better while doing so. This person prioritizes results, but also focuses on asking you questions in a way that makes you reflect, pushes you to get to the solutions yourself rather than giving you the answers at the first chance and has a review process that not only focuses on the delivery of the task/result but also on driving learning for you. These bosses, in a very intuitive way, are responsible for establishing the TMRR framework in you in your foundational years. Of course, they push for the target and the measurement, but the review they do is not just for results but also for learning. They build the reflection habit in you by asking the uncomfortable and challenging questions, especially

'What could you have done better?' They are the catalysts in converting the time you spend at work into an experience algorithm for you without you realizing it and, more importantly, in establishing the framework in your head for effective TMRR for the rest of your career. The other type of boss ensures that you deliver the results—you might even get a promotion because of that—but they do not aid your conversion of time into experience and they are not enablers in establishing the TMRR algorithm in your head. They have not made a permanent positive difference to you; they have simply been managers for a time.

The second thing that good bosses do is realize that major learning cycles are not just transformational opportunities for delivering superior business performance but equally transformational opportunities for developing their teams. When such an opportunity comes, you can almost see them going into high gear in how they involve and engage their teams, and ensuring that their teams and subordinates get as much out of the major learning cycle as the organization does.

Not Just Mr Nice

This brings us to a question I am often asked, which is, 'Who is a good boss?' and an opportunity to debunk a popular myth. A good boss is often confused with a nice person, a person who makes you feel good, is caring, speaks pleasantly and comes across as what can be described as a 'nice, decent' person. All these qualities are highly desirable in a good boss, but this is not what you are after in your foundational years. In those years, you are interested in a boss who builds your algorithm, who helps you expand your capacities by challenging you to operate beyond your comfort zone, who can ask you the uncomfortable question 'What can you do better?' and who does not allow you to get into a comfort zone. Now, in your foundational years, if you get somebody who can do this and is also a nice person, fantastic, but sometimes that's like asking for utopia. In the foundational years, if I ever have to make a choice between a nice person who does not build my algorithm and somebody who seems like a very tough person, who makes me feel uncomfortable, but who is continuously building my algorithm and stretching me and expanding what I am capable of— then, any day, I would choose the second person. In your foundational years, evaluate a good boss based on what they do for your algorithm, what permanent good change they bring in you, and less by whether they make you 'feel good'. I of course do not want the bosses who are reading this book to interpret this as a license to not be nice. Being nice is a good human quality which all of us must aim for.

Is It Just Luck, Then?

This, then, brings us to the fundamental question—if a good boss in the foundational years is so important for long-term career success, then how does one get a good boss? That's almost like saying that a lot of career success is dependent on good luck rather than what you do. As it is said, there are only two things you can't choose in your life—your parents and your bosses. As an aside, it means that for everything else that you feel unhappy about in your life, it's a choice you made, so don't externalize it. If a boss is so important for long-term career success, then is luck the driver of career success? Is it that more successful people are simply those who were lucky to have had great bosses in their foundational years and less successful people simply those who were unlucky to have had less effective bosses? Yes, there is an element of luck and serendipity in the bosses you get, there is no denying that. But equally, there is a lot that you have in your own hands, and I want to describe what you can do to catalyse the probability that you have a good boss in your foundational years.

In a way, this is a chance to practise one of the things we discussed in chapter 4 on productivity. Whether or not you get a good boss is in your circle of concern, and as we discussed, the best way to deal with what is in your circle of concern is to find paths to it through your circle of influence. Let us then see what the possible paths to getting a good boss through your circle of influence are. There are three, and these are all things that you can do, things that are within your influence and not a matter of chance.

What You Seek Is Seeking You

Pathway no. 1 to getting a good boss is to be a good subordinate. Just as each one of us is looking out for a good boss, good bosses are looking out for good subordinates.

They are looking for people who can implement their vision, who have the drive to deliver results and who have the initiative and capability to operate independently. If you can be a good subordinate, you will be noticed by the good bosses in your ecosystem. Good bosses also have a lot of leverage in the organizations they work in. If they spot a good subordinate, they have the leverage and influence to get that subordinate working for them in their team soon.

I have personally, in my capacity as a boss, done this often, and yes, I do consider myself a 'good' boss. Once, I had a very young brand manager working in my team on an important new launch. This person did a good job and was a great subordinate, as I described above. Hence, when a chance came up later for a more prestigious role in my organization, a role that I considered critical to driving the growth vision I had for my business, I had no doubt that this person was the right one for the job. Having spotted a good subordinate, I ensured that this person worked with me directly or indirectly in the coming years. Assuming that I was a good manager and leader, I was significantly enhancing that person's chance of success in their long-term career by giving them an opportunity to work closely with me for a long duration in the foundational years.

Work in Companies with Good Bosses

Pathway no 2 to getting a good boss is to work in organizations where there is a higher probability that more bosses are 'good' bosses. If there is a company where 30 per cent of the managers are good bosses and another where 70 per cent of the managers are good bosses, then obviously, the probability of getting a good boss is higher in the second company. People often ask, how do you know which company has a higher percentage of good bosses? I think there are a series of generic indicators suggestive of whether a company has more good bosses or not, and it would be advisable to look for these indicators in the career choices you make in your foundational years. The first indicator is the company's standing in the talent market. If it has a reputation for hiring high-quality talent, then it has a higher probability of having more good bosses. The other indicator is the importance the company places on the development of its people. Are the managers in the company evaluated only on the results they produce or are they also evaluated on how they develop and groom their people? This indicator would be difficult to make out from the outside, but if you are making a career choice, then it is important to make a few reference check calls to insiders to understand this aspect. Hence, a vital part of career decision-making is determining which companies one should work for in the foundational phase of your career.

In this context, I am often asked whether a person in the foundational phase of his or her career should work in start-ups or in more established businesses. There is no easy answer to this since both have its pros and cons. The pros of working in start-ups are that there is a lot more entrepreneurial opportunity, the opportunity to create things for the first time, the opportunity to learn by doing and, last but not least, the possibility of creating wealth through stock options if the company becomes highly successful. The cons of working in start-ups are that by nature, start-ups are in a phase where they are chasing delivery of results for their own long-term survival, and so the managers and bosses there are mainly managing subordinates for result delivery rather than maximizing learning and development. Equally, because of the compelling need to deliver results, there can be situations where the managers are less willing to give subordinates space to make mistakes and learn. They are more hands-on in such spaces, with less empowerment of subordinates as a result. Hence, I would recommend that you consider these pros and cons in the context of the stage of your career and then make an informed decision.

Ride the Good Luck

The third pathway to getting a good boss is an interesting one. Sometimes, by sheer good luck, we end up with good bosses. Good bosses are gold dust and if you do end up with one, it is worthwhile to make career choices to try and prolong working with that boss. This is particularly important in your foundational years. I have deployed this strategy again and again and I do believe I have gained very much by doing that.

Hence there are three clear pathways, three things you can do to improve the probability of getting a good boss in your foundational years. These are—being a good subordinate, working in companies that have a higher percentage of good bosses and hanging on to good bosses when you find them. Each one of these is within your influence, these are things you can catalyse, and these are not a matter of chance. And given how important a good boss in the foundational years is to long-term career success, I would urge each one of you to actively try these three paths and catalyse your real individual growth and career success. One last thing—the term 'boss' is often used only for the immediate manager, but the way I see it, it is more than that. It also covers others in the hierarchy, which could be the manager's manager and others who are as relevant, as all these people impact the algorithm development of employees in the organization.

My Bosses and the Impact They Had on Me

In my own career, two of my bosses, Bharat Puri and Anand Kripalu, have played an extraordinary role in driving my real individual growth and helping me succeed. Bharat was my first boss in Asian Paints after my trainee stint, and he was a great role model on how to balance the hard and the soft, how to balance task orientation and a human touch, how to think consumer and brands, and so on. He kept giving me 'stretch projects' whenever possible, and gave me the space to have a point of view, express myself and be a voice on the table even when I was very young. I worked with him for the first seven years of my career, a fairly defining foundational seven years. Then he went his own way and I went mine, tasting success with the skills he had helped me develop. Then, after many years, the opportunity to work together again came when I joined Cadbury, and that decision was motivated by the desire to work with Bharat again, an example of hanging on to good bosses when you find them. I joined Cadbury, but soon life took an unexpected twist—Bharat was moved to Singapore, and Anand joined the company in his place. That started an eight-year relationship with Anand as my boss. From him, I learnt the power of vision and ambition, and the willingness to stretch and put your neck on the line while encouraging others to be ambitious too. I learnt from him the ability to be highly strategy-focused, to choose what you do and, most importantly, to lead an organization through personal values and charisma. These two gentlemen—thorough leaders and bosses both—have been truly impactful in how they drove real growth in me. I have absolutely no doubt that a fair part of my success is thanks to these two bosses, and now friends, for having shown the way.

The other important person who can help create long-term career success is a mentor. Mentors, mentorship and so on are often abused words, used loosely for everything and anything starting from a friendly chat and advice to deep coaching. I don't want to get into defining mentorship. But I do want to point out the importance of good mentors for long-term career success.

The key challenge in today's world is that career planning is not as linear, as predictable or as safe as it was maybe a few decades ago. We do live in a VUCA world, not just from a business environment lens but also from a people career lens. Today, there are several choices that people are confronted with in their careers, and many of these are non-predictable, non-linear career choices. Many of these career choices are forks where one way can lead to long-term success while the other can possibly be highly detrimental to it. I have seen a lot of people with high potential fail to achieve the career success they deserved simply because they made the wrong career choices and then never recovered from them. I feel over half the career choices people make are possibly not the right ones for their long-term real individual growth and career success. These choices, however, look right when evaluated in the short-term and with the limited experience and judgement people have in the first halves of their careers. This is where a mentor comes in. The primary role of a mentor is to help you make choices that maximize the probability of long-term career success. In a VUCA world, with complex career choices, mentors are important to help make this choice, because many times, it is not easy to get it right all by yourself.

Who Is a Mentor?

This brings us to the question, who should be a mentor? There is a tendency to be flexible and, if I may say so, to be loose with this. There are three characteristics I would advise you to look for in a mentor:

1. A mentor is necessarily senior to you, not a peer or somebody of similar profile, but somebody who is distinctly ahead of you in the career curve. The reason for this is that you expect a mentor to provide a different view of your career from the one you have. Let's visualize your forty-year career as a 40 km-long road you are travelling on. Let us say you have worked for ten years and hence your view of your career is looking forward from the ten-year point towards the next thirty years in a forty-year career. In that thirty-year view, maybe the next few years can be visualized, but thereafter, it becomes difficult to visualize clearly. Let us say your mentor has worked for twenty years, and has two views of your career. For the 10–20-year path, your mentor has a view looking backwards, a view different from yours. For the 20–40-year phase, they have a view looking forward. Fundamentally, this means you are able to get two views to making a

career decision—your view, which is a view looking forward, and your mentor's, which is a combination of looking forward and backwards. Your mentor's different view can give you a perspective on your career choices that may not be apparent to you. You cannot get this different view if your mentor is not senior to you or ahead of you in the career path. Your peers and friends often have a similar profile and their advice is useful in making career choices, but it is often from a view which is similar to yours. A good mentor's advice is invaluable in making the right career choice because of the different view they bring.

2. A mentor is necessarily someone who knows you well and hence does not give generic career advice, but gives advice based on a good understanding of you. A good way of thinking is that you don't want a career counsellor, but somebody who deeply understands you, what drives you, your strengths and motivations, what you can be successful in, and hence is able to provide you a perspective with that in-depth understanding of you.

3. A mentor should not be in your line of authority and leadership. That's because you don't want the mentor to have a conflict between their allegiance to the organization, their own interests and what is right for you. You want a mentor to advise you from only one lens—what is good for you in the longer term—with no other conflict of interest.

It is clear from these characteristics that good mentors can't be found one fine day, but must be cultivated over time. It requires an investment from your side to cultivate that relationship in a selfless way for long-term benefits. I have seen many people neglect sustaining the relationship with prospective mentors and when there is a need to make an important career decision, there is an absence of that truly trusted and capable mentor. You cannot expect your mentor to be available to you at a time you need to make a decision if you have not kept in touch for a few years.

I want to give examples of the kind of mistakes good mentors can help avoid. The first one is a common mistake I see people commit in their foundational years—to not put themselves out there. They tend to not take the stretch assignment, to not do the highly operational, intensive role and to prefer more comfortable, qualitative and strategy-inclined roles. I remember how an HR person once quit because she was sent as an HR manager to a unionized factory. Coming from the corporate office, with its comfortable atmosphere and frequent interactions with senior management, the change to a more difficult factory environment was challenging, where most of the time your interaction is with blue-collar workers and a lot of time is spent resolving problems like canteen food, bus timings, etc. And she quit, not realizing that this experience was crucial to her foundation-building and temperament-building for being an HR leader one day.

However, this would never have been apparent to her from where she was; it would require a mentor she trusted to guide her through that decision.

The other kind of career mistake I have seen, which a good mentor can help avoid, is allowing the short term to cloud decision-making. A challenging few months can sometimes drive people to make poor decisions—they get pressured, sometimes to the point of being desperate, and make poor career choices. Or they might just be tempted by whatever looks good. E.g. when it is widely reported in the news that a start-up has just raised big money, youngsters decide to join it just because it looks like the 'in thing' at that time. Helping people make decisions that are good for the long term, without being swayed by short-term stimuli, is a role that mentors can play.

Unleash the Catalyst

1. External stakeholders like your bosses and mentors are tremendous catalysts for real individual growth and long-term career success.
2. There are three things you can do, that are in your influence, to improve the chance that you get a good boss—being a good subordinate, working in companies which have a higher percentage of good bosses and hanging on to good bosses when you find them.
3. Mentors are critical to ensuring that you make the right career decisions in an increasingly VUCA-filled

business and career world. Finding the right mentor is important, and when you find the right one, cultivating your relationship with them over time is critical.

8

Long Stints at One Company and the Decision to Quit

One of the most challenging career management decisions is the decision to quit from your current job and company, to either join another organization or to start your own venture. As I mentioned in the previous chapter, I have seen many people not achieve career success commensurate with their real potential. As I observed these people's careers, in many cases, I found that the underachievement was quite often due to poor career decisions and, in most cases, a poorly thought through decision on when to quit. A single poor decision on when to quit can have a very high impact on your long-term career success.

A related question is, how long should one work in one company? Often, I find, especially among younger people, the feeling that working too long in one company might be detrimental to one's career. They see their friends hop around and sometimes they also consider change just because they feel they have worked too long in one place. The decision to quit might be rationalized and justified by a hundred other reasons, but often, the real underlying reason is the sense that I have worked too long here and now it is time to change. These are among the poorest career decisions I have seen.

So how long should one work in one company, one organization? The answer to that question lies in what it is doing to your real individual growth, your experience algorithm. Is the long stint helping you solidify your experience algorithm or has it started to stagnate at some stage? In my own judgement, long stints in one company are highly beneficial to the experience algorithm. Let me explain why.

At any given point of time, when you are in a job, you are learning from that job and your experience algorithm is being built based on the job/role you are doing. What happens when you have a long stint in one organization is that after a point of time, you are learning not just from the role/job that you are currently doing but from all the previous roles that you did in that organization. Let me explain with my own experience.

In my stint with Mondelez, which was over eleven years long, I had the privilege of being closely associated with two brands—Cadbury Silk and Oreo. I had the opportunity to work on these brands in their formative launch years, and without sounding arrogant, I would say that these two brands are possibly among the best new product successes the Indian FMCG sector has

seen in this decade. The first time I worked on these
brands was when I was heading the chocolate and
biscuit categories between 2010 and 2013. In that stint,
I was closely involved in launching/growing these
brands, and it was extremely rewarding to see the
scorching pace of growth both the brands had during
this tenure. Thereafter, I moved out of this role into
another one that was in the Asia–Pacific region, and my
direct line of sight of these brands was limited. After
a few years, I came back as managing director, India.
When I returned, I again had direct line of sight to these
two brands, and I could assess the performance of both
the brands and, more importantly, analyse the current
performance with the lens of actions I had taken in my
previous stint. With the discipline of TMRR, I asked
myself, 'What did I do in the formative stages of these
brands that still have an impact on their performance
even after a few years?' And most importantly, 'What
could I have done better at the formative stage?' The
answers to these questions helped me in further
building my experience algorithm on new product
launches.

To put it simply, as managing director, I was learning
and building my algorithm not just from my job as MD,
but also from a role I had done in the same company
as category director, chocolates and biscuits, 3–4 years
ago. It meant that my experience algorithm was being
built at a rapid scale; it was not just being built on what
I was doing at that time, but on what all I had done in

the same company for over a decade. That, in a way, is the simple benefit of a long stint in one company— once you cross the critical mass of years, say, five years, you are not just learning from the role/job you do but also from all the previous roles you have done in that company.

Normally, when you are in a job, your experience algorithm is being built based on that role—one can call it the linear curve of building experience. But when the learning is not just limited to what you are doing at that point of time, when you are learning and building the experience algorithm from all that you have done in the past in that company, the algorithm-building becomes a non-linear, exponential curve. I have had the privilege of two decadal stints in two companies, and at both these places, the decade-long time meant that I definitely had the exponential algorithm-building and very rapid experience-building in the second five years of the decade I spent in those companies.

Would that mean one should not quit at all and work all their life in the same company? There are some cases where I have seen people work in one company all their lives and end up with highly successful careers. But very few people have careers like that. So while I do advocate long stints in organizations, I equally want to help you make the right career choices if you do want to change organizations. There are a set of career decision-making guidelines and thoughts that I want to leave you with in this chapter.

Most careers do involve the decision to quit and the decision to join another place. An important question to consider in this context is: are the decision to quit and the decision to join two different decisions or are these parts of one decision? Treating these two as part of the same decision is often where many people falter in their careers. In my understanding, quitting and joining elsewhere are separate decisions and must be taken independent of each other. That means that the decision to quit has to be taken first, and must be taken independent of the decision on where to join.

In a country like India, and indeed, in many other countries, opportunity is not the constraint. At any given point of time, there is an opportunity out there that looks and feels like it is better than what you are doing right now. Is the relative attraction of that opportunity compared to your current role a good enough reason for you to quit your current organization? Among the poorest career decisions I have seen people make is the decision to quit as a consequence of the decision to join. There are always better opportunities outside at any point of time—that is not reason enough to quit. Taken to the extreme, you can do it once in a while, quit because you found something better. But suddenly, at some stage, the opportunities dry up for such a person. More importantly, the process of foundation-building and experience algorithm-building can take a severe knock because of the unnecessary change.

If one were to make the decision to quit independently and make it first, preferably even before you start searching for opportunities, then how should one make the decision to quit? If you want to quit, then you have to have the right reasons to quit, not reasons to join elsewhere. To give an analogy, one must have strong supply-side reasons to quit, not demand-side reasons of joining elsewhere. And according to me, the default mode is not to quit, it is to stay. There must be credible reasons to quit, rather than the default being to quit and then finding reasons to stay.

So what then would be credible reasons to quit? I believe there are only two credible reasons that can allow you to take the 'quit' decision—learning and fit. If at some stage, you feel you are no longer learning and your algorithm is not building up, and you are sure that it is because of the organization and not because of you, then you can consider quitting your current organization. The second aspect is 'fit'. When you feel your values and culture no longer match those of the organization and you are fundamentally a misfit in your current organization, that is the time to quit. These are the only two reasons that should drive your reason to quit. It should not be pay, designation and other emotional aspects. Most of these reasons will come up again and again in your career, and will tend to fix themselves if you build your algorithm and perform. But when the learning starts to stagnate or when you experience a serious fit issue, you should consider quitting.

It is important to examine these in detail and be sure that these factors are real, not a result of rationalization. Sometimes, people experience negative triggers—it could be a bad project, a new boss whom you don't like at a personal level, a bad quarter of performance, etc. These triggers sometimes make you feel that there is not enough learning and that you don't fit. It is important when you make the decision that you are able to isolate the current negative trigger you are experiencing from the more fundamental issues of learning and fit. Triggers will come and go, including in the new place that you join, so you have to be sure about the fundamental reasons for your decision.

The two common 'quit' mistakes I have seen are getting tempted by an external opportunity and quitting without having a fundamental reason to leave and confusing short-term negative factors in your current organization with fundamental, long-term reasons to quit. In most such cases, people make the decision first and then create the reasons for the justification/ rationalization of the decision. Career change decisions like quitting your current company are among the most important decisions you will make. You must not fall into a trap of poor decision-making—making decisions first and then finding the reasons to justify them. You must objectively evaluate the reasons first and then come to the decision.

In my career, I have had the opportunity to guide and mentor many people, and most of the cases I have had to deal with have been related to the two quit mistakes above. The technique I have used most often to help such people evaluate the objectivity of their decision is something I want to describe using the diagram below.

My current organization 'What is good'	My future organization 'What can be good'
My current organization 'What is bad'	My future organization 'What can be bad'

As you can see, it is a classic 2/2 matrix. On one axis is my current organization and my future organization and on the other is 'what is good' and 'what is bad'. This gets you the four quadrants as described in the diagram above. When people first make the decision to quit and then find the reasons to justify and rationalize it, what tends to happen is that they actually see only two quadrants properly. Those two quadrants are 'My current organization—What is bad' and 'My future organization—What can be good'. In many ways, this is a symptom of a superficial, poorly made decision— when only two quadrants have been thought about by the decision-maker. Often in my role as a guide and mentor, I get people to first realize that they have not thought with equal depth about all the four quadrants, and then I get them to think about the two quadrants they have missed. Getting them to a state of mind where they are not finding reasons to justify a decision already made, but to objectively consider all the four quadrants and then make the decision, is what I try to ensure so that they make the right decision for their long-term career success.

Every time you decide to change organizations, a way of evaluating if you have made a good decision or a superficial decision is to analyse the four quadrants. If you find that you are very clear about the two quadrants that justify the decision to quit and take the new opportunity, but are struggling to meaningfully fill the other two quadrants that would push you to stay, then that is a symptom of a decision that has been made first and then rationalized. A good quit decision would be one where you are able to fill all the four boxes clearly and fairly, and the quit decision still holds.

Having described the four-quadrant technique, I still want to go back to my original premise that the decision to quit must be taken independent of the decision to join, and ideally before the decision to pursue opportunities outside your current organization. The four-quadrant technique is applicable only when you have not done that, and hence end up in a situation where you have to make a decision to quit when you have already got a new opportunity lined up to join. I do want to clarify here that I am talking of the decision to quit and not actual quitting. Actual quitting is something you can do either at the time you make the decision to quit or after you find a new opportunity—that is your choice.

Let's assume that you have made the decision to 'quit' independent of and prior to the decision to 'join'. What then should be the guidelines on where to join? What I have observed is that most people make the 'join' decision based on pay, designation, role, career prospects, reputation of the prospective company, etc. If we were to go back to our core principle—that what drives long-term career success is real individual growth—then is it not important that the opportunity and environment for real individual growth be considered important criteria in the 'join' decision? Please make sure you evaluate the new opportunity based on how effective it will be in building the experience algorithm, how likely it is to provide you major learning cycles and how likely you are to get good bosses there who would build your foundation and drive your learning. These are more important aspects in evaluating the 'join' decision than pay, designation and career prospects.

The other key dimension to consider in the 'join' decision is the 'fit' dimension. I find that people underemphasize the importance of this softer dimension compared to the harder ones. Most people mistakenly assume that if you are successful in one environment, then you would be equally successful in all environments. This is not the case. Most of us are wired to succeed more in some environments/cultures than others. Very few women and men can succeed in all environments. I have made this mistake once and realized it the hard way. Equally, I have seen others make this mistake. Many years ago, I had an absolute superstar working in my team who quit and joined a company that was much more reputed on paper. In two years, that person was struggling to deliver any impact in the new company and his career took a knock, which was difficult to compensate for in the future. So my sincere request is, please make an effort to understand how good a fit you are in the new company and environment. Is the culture there going to be a tailwind for your success or is it going to be a serious headwind, given the kind of person you are? And do not ignore signals that say you won't fit—you can be assured that they will come back and bite you later.

My Quit and Join Decisions

I want to describe some of the quit and join decisions I made in my life as examples for readers to understand good and bad decisions. I started in Asian Paints and spent close to a decade there. My decision to quit the company was a poor one. Firstly, I made the mistake of not making the quit decision independent of the join decision. The quit decision was driven by a fancy title and pay from GE Countrywide, a consumer finance company. The fundamental reasons to quit Asian Paints were absent. I was experiencing tremendous learning there and had a great 'fit' with the culture and values. Equally, on top of a poor quit decision, I took a poor join decision, in which I did not evaluate my fit with the new company. It was apparent to me on joining that I had zero fit with that company, which had a very different culture and values.

The next career decision, hence, was to quit GE Countrywide and join Mirc Electronics (Onida). The quit decision was obvious, as stated above, due to the lack of fit, but the join decision was not easy for me. I had two offers, one from Onida and the other from a more pedigreed, reputed organization, but for a slightly lower-level job. I did agonize over the join decision, and finally chose Onida for the higher scale and complexity the role provided, which I thought would help my algorithm-building. And it was proven right as I built tremendous experience there.

I spent four years in Onida and then made the quit decision well before the join decision, well before I started looking for opportunities. The quit decision was driven by learning stagnation, as I knew that in Onida, a promoter organization with a permanent CEO, I had limited opportunities to progress to higher-order, more complex roles for my learning, and that I would be doing the same job that I had done for the previous four years in the future as well. Having made the quit decision independently, I then made the join decision with Cadbury. Again, it was a decision based on learning and fit. I knew Cadbury would provide real individual growth opportunities. I also knew that I had a tremendous fit with the culture, having known many people there. I emphasized learning and fit and hence, did not hesitate to move at a lateral level to Cadbury, as I knew that once learning and fit fall in place, everything else follows.

Unleash the Catalyst

1. Career decisions, including the decision to change companies, are among the most important decisions you will take and usually impact how successful you are in your career. The right decisions will maximize real individual growth and the wrong decisions will curtail it.

2. In that context, I do believe long stints in the same company are highly beneficial to the experience algorithm-building because the experience curve moves from being a linear curve to an exponential curve in long stints.

3. The decision to quit your current organization and the decision to join a new one are two different decisions. They are best made independent of each other. Ideally, the decision to quit must be made even before you start to explore and consider outside opportunities.

4. The decision to quit your current organization should be driven by the fundamental reasons of learning and fit. Learning is about saying your experience algorithm growth has slowed down and fit is about values and culture. Other reasons like pay, designation and negative triggers like a temporary bad phase should have a lower weightage in the quit decision.

5. The four quadrant technique is a good way of evaluating if you have made a sound decision or if you have made the decision first and then found reasons to justify it.

6. For the join decision, evaluating prospective learning
    and fit in the new company is more important than
    pay and other prospects. Will the new place accelerate
    your real individual growth? Will the new place have
    a culture and value system where you will fit in and
    find it easy to deliver in?

Unleashing the Catalyst: Summarizing Parts I and II and Setting Up Part III

In Part I, we have covered the means to driving real individual growth. The three important concepts in this context are:

1. Converting time into experience is the very bedrock of real individual growth. An effective TMRR model is the key to converting the time you are spending at work into an experience algorithm that will drive your success in the future.
2. Applying the TMRR algorithm on major learning cycles is an exponential way to drive real individual growth.
3. Just building the experience algorithm is not enough; you have to, in parallel, increase your productivity. Productivity is the means through which you can convert the experience algorithm into results. The key to growing productivity is to focus on the circle of influence and to make sure you allocate your time to the rocks.

However, fantastic real individual growth has to be backed by good career management decisions and approach. The key to that is to make career decisions based on what drives real individual growth.

In Part II, we covered what the key principles to this end are:

1. In careers, win when it matters—which is the second half. It is possible to win in the second half only if

you do foundation-building and drive real individual growth in the first half.

2. To do foundation-building in the first half, make career choices that focus on depth over width, ensure completion of major learning cycles and get out there when you can.

3. Getting good bosses is crucial to foundation-building, and mentors are crucial in making the right decisions in the VUCA world of careers and business.

4. Long stints in one company can have a positive and exponential impact on building your experience algorithm.

5. The decisions to quit your current company and join elsewhere are crucial and must be done right. To get them right, focus on separating the quit decision from the join decision. The quit decision must be based on the absence of learning and fit in your current workplace. The join decision must be based on opportunities for real individual growth and the potential fit, not title or pay or other trappings.

If you make career decisions based on the above principles, based on always asking what will help drive real individual growth, you will make good career decisions.

The combination of a powerful experience algorithm, high productivity and good career decisions can set you up for extraordinary career success. That brings us to the last, but very important, section of the book. We have all heard of the work–life equation. One of my firm beliefs is that the life part of work–life has a huge impact on the success people achieve in the work part. It is a highly erroneous notion that success at work is only because of what you do at work. Part III will talk about how you can make your life a catalyst to help you achieve more success at work and, indeed, in life.

PART III

9

The Power of Life as a Catalyst

'Work–Life balance' is a much bandied about term, and often used loosely without adequate rigour. It is a term which, while being neutral in its wording, is often used to connote how work takes away from life and how, to preserve the balance, it is important to work less and have more of a life. This term has almost always been used in a one-dimensional way in which it conveys the impact of work on life. It is seldom used in a more holistic way, which not only covers the impact of work on life but also covers the reverse—the impact of life on work. In my experience, the impact of work on life is much less than the impact of life on work.

Firstly, let me start by explaining why I think so. When we think of the impact that work has on life and try to improve the work–life balance, we are focused on a few key things. First and foremost, most people try to reduce the time they spend at work in order to find more time to spend with the family and on what they refer to as more 'meaningful' things. In essence, the work–life balance often comes down to whether you can find a few extra hours per week to spend with the family. The other aspect of work–life balance, which many people try to manage, are the stress and pressure at work, and how to ensure that these do not negatively impact life. Both these are good objectives and definitely worth pursuing. However, let us explore the other side of it, which is the impact of life on work. Life is the force that defines your personality and how you come across as a person at work—the values, beliefs, integrity and other human characteristics you bring daily to work. I am entirely convinced that these 'life characteristics' have a huge impact on how successful a person is at work. Hence it is my conviction that the impact of life on work is fundamental to success at work, while the impact of work on life is limited to a few hours more for life per week. I strongly believe that the impact of life on work is more important, and each one of us must focus on how we lead our lives and see how that catalyses how successful we are at work.

One of the most important anecdotes on this comes from the life of Albert Einstein, the celebrated Nobel Prize–winning giant of the world of science. Einstein, as the story goes, was a passionate violin player. More importantly, he believed that the fact that he was a violin player positively impacted his ability to be a successful scientist. For most of us, it is difficult to explain how playing the violin or, for that matter, any musical instrument, can bring about success as a scientist. However, one would assume that a person of Einstein's intellect and scientific temper would have had some reason for believing that playing the violin helped him be a better scientist. Maybe it taught him to be more patient when pursuing complex problems whose solutions were not evident. Maybe it allowed him to make more abstract connections between unrelated things, which helped create insights. Maybe it simply helped him concentrate better when he was at work. Finding an explanation is both difficult and, to be honest, unimportant; life is a lot more complex than that. However, the fact that life has a high degree of impact on work, in a variety of ways and on every single minute we spend at work, is a truism that does not need a lot of validation.

There are many ways life impacts work and success at work. Life impacts work by shaping our personality, our values, our integrity, our characteristics, our friendliness, our behaviour with other colleagues and so on. I will not attempt to cover the impact of life in all these dimensions; it is too complex a topic. However, just because the impact of life on work is complex and difficult to understand, it does not mean you let life play out. Assuming that it automatically impacts work positively would be a mistaken assumption. We have to actively catalyse life for it to have a positive impact on success at work.

There are two critical aspects of life I would like to focus on, which I believe would be the focus areas for each one of us to actively catalyse success at work. These are:

1. Developing a hobby you are passionate about.
2. Deepening your value system and developing lodestar values.

10

A 'Passionate Striving' Hobby as a Catalyst

One of the important effects of life on work can be seen when you develop a 'passionate striving' hobby in your life. I chanced upon this insight through my own life and by observing others over many years. I started running seriously about a decade ago, and have run a couple of half-marathons. When I first began running, I noticed that many senior and successful people from the corporate sector were into running, and many ran with a degree of passion and commitment that was commendable.

Then I started playing golf. I noticed that there were many senior corporate heads playing golf too, and again, with a degree of passion that was incredible to see. Of late, I have seen people take up cycling, a sport that seems to be growing in leaps and bounds, with people setting off on 50 km bike rides at 4.30 in the morning. Again, I have been seeing a similar pattern—many successful corporate leaders taking up this sport with great passion. Mountaineering is another sport that is popular with the highly successful set.

As I observed this trend, I wondered why so many senior and successful people were gravitating to such sports. One does not often hear that the legendary CEO of a large company has suddenly started playing table tennis at the age of fifty-five, but you would often hear of a CEO who has run a full marathon and is now preparing to run the ultra-marathon. There was a pattern in this trend—all these sports, be it running, cycling, golf or mountaineering, were mostly individual sports; these are not what you would characterize as team sports. The other interesting thing about these sports is that you don't necessarily play these to win. These sports are mostly about competing with yourself, continuously trying to improve, competing against your previous best and trying to get better incrementally all the time. I like to term these sports 'striving' sports, the kind where you have to keep working very hard and where you need a high degree of perseverance and commitment to stay where you are and improve incrementally. Striving sports are very different from recreational sports. If you were to visualize a billiards table in a very cool room with a glass of wine in your hand, you would get the picture of a recreational sport. You don't run a marathon for recreation or pleasure; it is a striving sport, even though you might feel good at the end of it.

As I saw these patterns of striving, of mainly individual sports, of mainly aiming at self-improvement and not winning, I kept wondering why. Why do these sports, and not any other, more conventional sports, seem to attract senior people from the corporate world? As I started unpeeling the onion of this answer, many insights and answers came to me. But the final breakthrough came when I started to understand motivations—the motivations of people at life and the motivations of people at work.

Most of us know Maslow's hierarchy, which explains the motivations of our life in a classic pyramid (figure reproduced below):

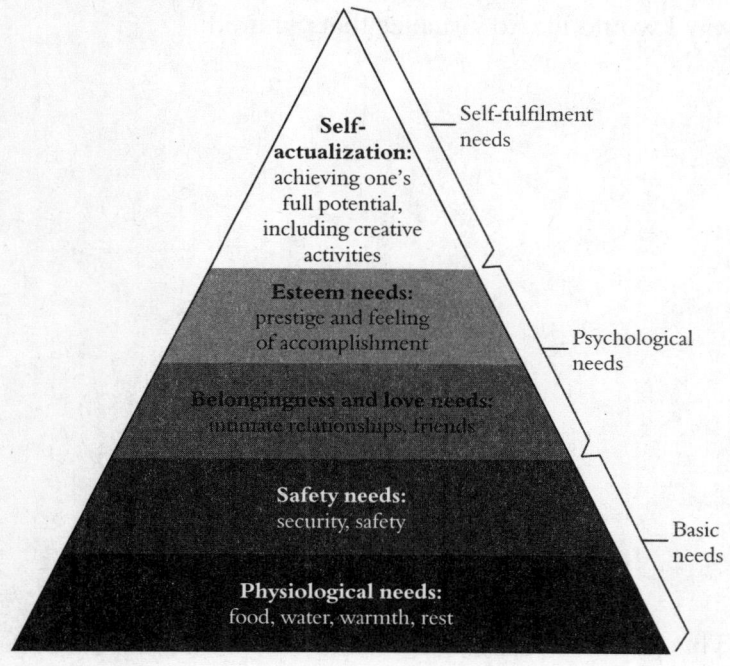

Maslow's hierarchy attempts to explain our motivations in life. It starts with our basic physiological and safety needs at the bottom of the pyramid and goes all the way to self-actualization—achieving our potential. These are the motivations that drive us, and each one of us is continuously trying to go higher in this pyramid.

While motivations in life were easier to understand given Maslow's hierarchy, I had to work hard to try and understand the motivations at work better for myself. In trying to understand this I was influenced by the work of David McClelland and Daniel Pink. A good way of thinking about it is to imagine it as a pyramid. This is the way I would like to visualize that pyramid:

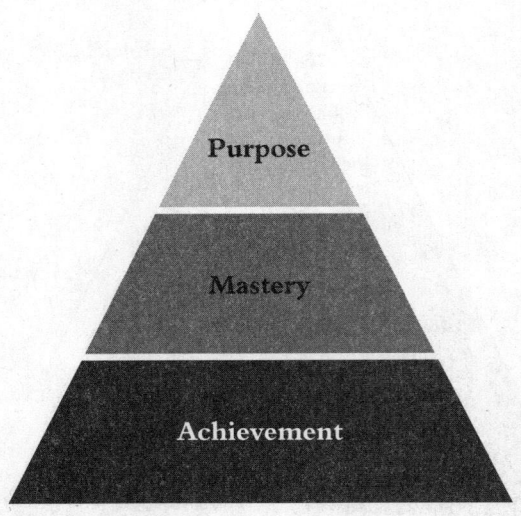

This pyramid explains what motivates us at work and in our careers. At the base of the pyramid is our need for achievement, our need to achieve material success and wealth, our need to achieve comfortable living standards for ourselves and for our families, our need to achieve respect and recognition, etc. A large portion of our careers is spent meeting our achievement need. The next level of motivation is mastery. This is our need for being the master of our trade, for the ability to say that what we do has our personal stamp of quality, a sense of representing a high standard of excellence in what we do, and for being a reference standard to the world in our area of work. The last and final motivation at the top of the pyramid is purpose. We are highly motivated by a sense of purpose at work that goes beyond our own achievements and mastery. This is about the 'why' of work, which is beyond our personal needs—the sense of having a cause, a vision, a purpose. The combination of achievement, mastery and purpose represents the motivations that drive us at work and in our careers.

There are similarities between Maslow's hierarchy, which explains the motivations of life, and the work pyramid, which explains our motivations at work. The primary similarity is that both are pyramids, the inference being that we start at the base of the pyramid and work our way to the top. The other similarity is the unsaid fact that the higher in the pyramid you operate, the better it is.

However, there is one fundamental difference between the two pyramids, and understanding that difference is crucial to understanding the impact of life on work. In Maslow's hierarchy, most of us have found it relatively easy to meet the needs of the base of the pyramid, namely, the physiological and safety needs. My guess is most readers of this book are from families that have provided for these needs in the early stages of their lives, and later on, they have found jobs, which means that they are not fighting to meet these basic needs. As we meet the basic needs, they can grow a bit, but they don't expand continually, so we can meet these needs and move on. This relatively easy conquest of the early part of Maslow's pyramid means that a greater part of our lives are focused on the motivations in the middle and the top of the pyramid.

This is where the work motivations pyramid is fundamentally different. At the base of the work pyramid is the achievement need, a need which I like to call a hungry beast. I call it a beast because this need keeps growing— the more you achieve, the more you need to achieve. Unlike Maslow's hierarchy, where you can satisfy the physiological and safety needs and then move on to the next level, in the work pyramid, the achievement need is a hungry beast. It cannot be satiated easily. The more you feed it, the more it grows. That means it is more difficult to move on and operate at the next levels of motivation, namely, mastery and purpose.

This is particularly paradoxical in the way it manifests in senior people, folks who have achieved something worthwhile in their careers and hence are now in positions of importance and seniority. At senior levels, one of the critical drivers of success is leadership— how you engage, motivate and lead others is often the make-or-break for your success. To be able to motivate and engage others, it is important to operate from the levels of mastery and purpose. Mastery is what brings the teacher/coach out in a leader, which allows other people to learn and build their skills/capabilities. The leader's sense of purpose is often what gives the team the sense of a mission, the sense of doing something meaningful in their otherwise mundane work. Leaders who are focused on meeting their own achievement needs, and not operating from mastery and purpose, will be ineffective, often dysfunctional, leaders. Most of us at work have seen such dysfunctional leaders—senior people who are focused on furthering their own careers, their own success and achievements. Such leaders are often quite dysfunctional in managing their teams and are very poor leaders and motivators. In a way, the more they focus on their own success, the less successful they are, because they don't leverage the biggest driver for their success, which is their team. And this can often create a vicious cycle—the leader focuses on achieving more for himself or herself, which demotivates the team, which makes success even more difficult for the leader, which means they become even more self-achievement-driven, which demotivates the team further, and so on. Sometimes, these cycles develop to a point where the leader and the team actually become competitors. Such cycles often end only with either the exit of the leader or, at times, sadly, the exit of the entire team.

At a senior level, operating from a sense of mastery and purpose, and not focusing on your own achievements, is easy to say, but difficult to do. This is because most senior people reach senior positions because they have achieved a lot in their careers. In many ways, they are super achievers, which is the reason they get the senior jobs in the first place. It means their achievement need is very strong, it is a particularly hungry and overdeveloped beast, and that's why they've got to this senior level. Now, when they have to go beyond and operate from mastery and purpose, it becomes challenging, given how overdeveloped their achievement need is. Senior leaders who manage to reconcile and overcome this contradiction are the leaders who go on to achieve greater successes. So the core challenge is that what got them here, their achievement need, won't take them further. In fact, it will become a liability. This is the paradox to solve to catalyse leadership success.

Resolve the Paradox, the Role of the Striving Hobby

By now, you must be wondering, what does all this have to do with striving sports—running, cycling, golf, etc.? That is where this narrative started. I did mention earlier that I saw a pattern of senior people gravitating to such sports and showing remarkable commitment, passion and effort at self-improvement in these sports. And if you remember, the key characteristics of these sports were that these were individual sports, not team-oriented, there is really no clear win-lose and there is a degree of passionate striving required. I tried to find the reason for senior corporate folks gravitating to such sports, and that's when I found the connection to the pyramid of work motivations.

Successful senior leaders are those who manage to operate from mastery and purpose despite having an overdeveloped and hungry achievement need. One key way to resolve this paradox is to find alternate avenues to fulfil their achievement need, to find ways of feeding their hungry achievement beast outside work. That is where the striving sports come in. In a way, these senior leaders were finding ways of meeting their achievement need outside their work through these striving sports. The harder they try to reduce their next marathon timing by a few minutes, the more they are quenching their achievement need. The longer the bike ride they take over the weekend—and sometimes these rides are almost to the next city—the more they are pedalling to meet their achievement need. The more passionate they are in their goal of reducing their golf handicaps, the more they reduce their need for achievements at work. These striving sports are liberating them from having to meet all their achievement needs at work. And this liberation allows them to catalyse and activate their mastery and purpose motivations at work, making them greater leaders of their teams and organizations and, most importantly, making them more successful.

To validate this insight, I have one example, but I have a high degree of confidence in that one example—myself. I have observed my own evolution as a leader over many years. In the early to middle phase of my career, I was an achievement junkie, a super achiever. As I started to get to middle management and lower leadership positions, I started seeing the earliest signs of dysfunctionality in my leadership style. The simple symptom was that despite a lot of achievement, my team was not necessarily happy and motivated. However, I ploughed on, being a super achiever. In a strange way, my achievement orientation made me enrol myself in a half-marathon. I was in charge of getting colleagues from my then company to sign up for the marathon, and as the leader of that initiative, I felt I would be encouraging many people to join by leading from the front. So I started running, and given my achievement beast, naturally, I wanted to excel at the marathon also. The first time I ran the half-marathon, it took 2 hours and 52 minutes. The second time I ran, it was 2 hours and 20 minutes, a reduction of 32 minutes. Then I started playing golf and again, my super achiever kicked in. I used to relentlessly practise to improve, and reached a decent handicap very soon after I started playing. But more than my success at these sports, what I noticed was a gradual but sure change in my leadership style. I was less of an achievement junkie for my team at work. I was more motivating. I was coaching them, providing a vision and a sense of purpose. It was as if my desperation to succeed at work had reduced and I was truly driven by higher-order mastery and purpose motives at work. My own achievement was secondary. The beauty of this was that the less I focused on my own achievement, the more success I got at work. Some of my greatest career successes came about in this phase because my people were now a super-motivated and engaged team. We worked together with passion and for a cause, not for my achievement. Mentors who had known me over time could clearly see the changed, more motivating leader in me. I had changed materially for the better in a phase of five years. And I have no doubt that this change in my leadership effectiveness at work was catalysed by the passions in my life outside of work—running first, and then golf.

My dear readers, this change in me came about by sheer providence. However, for each one of you, there is an opportunity to actively catalyse this change to become a more effective leader. And the secret to that is to develop a 'passionate striving' hobby in life, one that gives you a sense of achievement and broadens your source of achievement beyond work. It should be a hobby in which you strive for achievement and one that liberates you from feeding the achievement need at work, and hence lets you graduate to mastery and purpose.

The question that I am immediately asked next is what qualifies as a 'passionate striving' hobby. Let's start with an example of what does not qualify as one—watching a lot of movies, even if you are passionate about it, because it does not give you a sense of achievement and it does not meet your achievement need. It might help you meet your entertainment need, your curiosity and knowledge need, or your need for social connectedness. A hobby can be considered 'passionate striving' only if it takes a lot of striving and helps meet your achievement need.

The most common striving hobbies are the ones I mentioned—running, mountaineering, cycling, golf. To this, I would add things like gardening, and social causes where you are trying to make a difference with a significant and consistent time commitment. Does a game of tennis every week for two intense hours with your buddy qualify as a 'passionate striving' hobby? I would lean towards no, the reason being that it might be meeting fitness and fun needs but not the achievement need. There is a difference between playing a tennis game every weekend for two hours and practising for the next marathon every weekend for two hours. Both are physically taxing, but the practice for the marathon is done with a determination to get better, to achieve better timings the next time, while the game of tennis is often played for fitness and fun. If you, however, do work continuously at tennis to get better, if you set yourself goals—like qualifying for the next level amateur tournament at your club—if you practise and play with an intensity to try and get better each time, then it can become a 'passionate striving' hobby that can help you meet your achievement need. But in the way most of us play weekend tennis, it does not. And I am using tennis here as an example for the many sports that people play. So to summarize, evaluate your hobby on these two criteria:

1. Is there a degree of striving involved?
2. Does it help meet your achievement need?

What, then, is the role of 'passionate' in the 'passionate striving' hobby that I talk about? Isn't this all about striving to build a sense of achievement? The role of passion is that you stay the course. Many people embark on striving hobbies, but they quickly drop them. They are unable to sustain them, and hence never get to the benefits I am talking about. However, if somebody is deeply passionate about that hobby, then they persevere at it and, hence, get the achievement benefits. So yes, after you read this book, many of you will start to dabble in hobbies. The question is, will you stay the course? And that is where I strongly advocate that you develop a degree of passion towards that hobby, so that there is a greater chance you continue and reap the benefits.

So folks, go out and build an interest or develop a hobby that you are passionate about that gives you a sense that you are achieving something. Then see how it changes you as a person at work and how much more successful you become as a result. Go for it!

Unleash the Catalyst

1. Motivations at work is defined by the pyramid comprising achievement, mastery and purpose. The key to succeeding at leadership is to operate at mastery and purpose at work and not be driven only by your need for achievement.
2. To operate at mastery and purpose you have to find a way of meeting your achievement need outside work. A 'passionate striving' hobby is the means to that.
3. It is important to be passionate about your hobby as otherwise you would not be able to sustain the striving for a long time.

11

Values as a Catalyst

One of the most important aspects of life is our values, which are at the very core of who we are. I find that people usually think of values primarily from the lens of character, i.e., they define the nature and character of a person. But to me, it is more than that. Values not only define who you are and what you do, but if catalysed effectively, can play a significant part in becoming an asset in your success tool kit. In the earlier chapters, we found the key to converting your algorithm and your productivity into catalysts for success. This chapter will help you convert your values into a catalyst for success.

If you go to any organization, work in any company, you often find a great deal of talk about values. There is a lot of emphasis on values—there are booklets, websites, events and forums dedicated to it. The importance of values is slowly but surely percolating down in the corporate world, and kudos to them for this progress. However, I find that in many places, corporate speak on values verges on the one-dimensional. In a way, what is continuously emphasized is that if you have poor values, you will not succeed and in some cases, you might even have to face disciplinary action. Hence, simply put, you are told subtly or directly that if you cheat, if you have a conflict of interest, if you indulge in any form of sexual or other harassment, if you misrepresent facts for your advantage, if you practise nepotism or favouritism, etc., then your career could be finished or at least severely impacted. However, there is not enough emphasis on the upside of good values. The focus tends to be primarily on the downside of a breach. There is no existing literature or culture that suggests that if you have excellent values or if you are a positive exemplar of good values, then all other things remaining equal, you have a higher chance of career success as compared to somebody who is more lax on values. Poor values have a downside, but the fact that good values have an upside is not spoken about enough.

It is not just about what is spoken, it is also about what is demonstrated. In most good companies, there would be demonstrated precedence that they don't tolerate any significant breach of values. There would be examples of people facing disciplinary action because they did something wrong. E.g. it is fairly common to see people losing their jobs because of having fudged their travel bills. While every wrongdoing might not have been caught, enough precedents exist in most organizations for it to be an effective deterrent. Like it is difficult to find discussion on the upside of good values, it is equally difficult to find demonstrated actions and precedents that reward good values. It is difficult to find people who had a career jump or promotion or a significant reward because they displayed exemplary values. E.g. it is difficult to find somebody who was a true champion of creating a diverse and inclusive environment actually being rewarded for that, despite the fact that organizations continuously emphasize diversity and inclusion. The incidents of being rewarded for exemplary demonstration of values are far fewer than demonstrated incidents of taking action on breach of values.

Limit the Downside, Leverage the Upside

Most of us have built an implicit understanding, an implicit coding, when it comes to values. Our implicit understanding is to avoid making a mistake on values. Years of said and unsaid aspects of corporate culture have established that implicit coding in most of us—limit the downside, don't take a risk with values and don't breach the established code. That is what I seek to change. I seek to change your understanding on values from a coding that says limit the downside to a coding that says leverage the upside. I am a firm believer that exemplary values can be a huge catalyst to success in careers and, indeed, in life. I do need to explain my conviction and the reasons for it, which I have analysed and developed over a fairly long period of time. And that conviction comes from my understanding of the positive impact that superior values have on a person's leadership potential.

As we go higher up in the corporate ladder, one of the key ingredients of success is leadership. I believe that superior values are the most important driver in generating that leadership potential. Leadership is a complex subject and often, the greatest challenge is in simply defining and measuring leadership. People confuse leaders and leadership. Leaders are often equal to people in senior positions in the company. The starting point to understanding this concept is to separate the position from leadership. If there are two vice presidents, that does not mean they automatically have the same leadership. They might be both called leaders in company parlance, though. How does one then determine who has greater leadership?

I like to measure leadership based on two metrics— followership and influence. Followership, as the word implies, is how large the number of their followers is and how strong the conviction of the followers is in following the leader. The greater the followership, the greater the leadership. A leader who has hundreds and thousands of followers, who all have tremendous belief and conviction in the leader, has much greater leadership than somebody who has fewer followers or who is unable to generate a strong conviction among them. Influence is about the extent of influence the leader has on their followership base. This combination of followership and influence is what, I believe, defines the strength of a person's leadership. The greater the leadership strength, the greater their followership and influence. Hereafter, whenever I refer to leadership in this chapter, I am talking of the combination of followership and influence. That is how I like to measure and define leadership.

Building Leadership

That automatically brings us to the question, how does one build leadership? What makes a strong leader? In my journey of developing this definition of leadership, quite early on, I found two key elements of building leadership and the commensurate followership and influence. Represented mathematically, it looked like this:

$$Leadership = Function (Position\ and\ Content)$$

Let me share a few thoughts on each of these. In the corporate world, there is no doubt that a person's position impacts the extent of leadership they can generate. Put simply, the higher the position of the person in the corporate ladder, the greater the opportunity for leadership. A more senior person starts with a degree of leadership which, as we defined, is the combination of followership and influence when they take on the senior role. Then they build on it or subtract from it based on what they do. So a new person taking on the role of a CEO starts with a degree of influence and followership, which is higher than what, say, a new VP starts with. This starting level of leadership is what inherently goes with the position—there is a degree of followership for each position and there is a degree of influence each position has. The more senior the position, the higher is the inherent starting-point followership and influence.

The second thing that builds leadership is the content of the leader. What does the leader say about strategies, what is his or her viewpoint on issues, what kind of decisions does he or she make and which causes does he or she make their own and fight for in the context of the business and the organization? These are the things that, over time, define the content of the leader, and the content either builds upon the followership and influence or diminishes it. For example, a CEO might believe that there is no space for small brands in the business, that these must be divested and bigger brands must be grown and nurtured. This is part of the CEO's content and guides what they say and do, and impacts the followership and influence they have. Similarly, a VP HR could have a content which is a belief on sharp differentiation based on talent and performance. So they have greater rewards for higher performers as opposed to a more democratic approach to this issue. This is a part of the VP HR's content, and impacts the followership and influence of this person.

Over time, as I observed leaders, I could definitely see that position and content had an impact on the leadership they generated. However, when I compared different leaders who had different levels of followership and influence, I found that these two factors, position and content, could explain only part of the difference in their followership and influence. I observed this particularly in leadership transitions—one leader moves on, a new person comes in and replaces the previous person in the same role, and you assess the leadership of the two over time. When I compared the leadership of the previous leader with that of the new one, I found a significant difference in their followership and influence. This was despite the fact that the position was the same and often, the content was very similar as well—they took similar decisions. Yet, there were massive differences in leadership. As I observed that, it became clear to me that position and content are necessary but not sufficient explanations for leadership differences. There was an X factor that explained the difference in the leadership that different people commanded, despite similar position and content.

In particular, I observed a set of leadership transitions very closely. To understand what drives this difference in leadership and the consequent impact on followership, I made a list of nine transitions, which I have personally been close to and have been able to observe over a meaningful period. These were nine situations where I saw one person being replaced by another in the same job. I had a ringside view to assess both the previous person and the new person. I first did the leadership level assessment. In each transition, I made an assessment of the followership and influence the earlier leader had. Then I made an assessment of the followership and influence the new leader was able to build after two years in the role. I then compared the leadership levels of the two leaders. Based on that, I was broadly able to categorize two types of transitions—one where the level of leadership of both the previous leader and the new leader was roughly the same and the other where the level of leadership of the two leaders had a significant difference. Since I wanted to understand the drivers of leadership, I focused primarily on the second type, where the level of leadership of the two leaders was very different.

As I studied the second type, I found that except in one case, where I could attribute the difference to content, in all the other cases, I was unable to attribute the difference in leadership to either position or content. One particular transition was very interesting. The previous leader was Smita and the new leader Rita, who was a team member of the previous leader and hence shared exactly the same beliefs on the content. In fact, Rita had helped develop much of the content of Smita and hence there was complete alignment on what they believed about the business. Yet, after two years, I found a staggering difference between the leadership the two had managed to generate. This sealed it in my mind— position and content are not the primary drivers of leadership.

I looked hard in this case, and then it came to me like a bolt from the blue—it was the difference in trust the two generated. It was all down to their values. One of them generated significant trust in the team and the wider organization, and hence commanded huge followership, while the other, while being outwardly friendly, generated less trust and hence could not build that much of a followership. The difference was in their values. Then

I applied this to the other transitions I studied and it fit again and again—values were the primary reason for the difference in leadership. Hence, it became clear to me that the leadership equation was now a function of three variables: position, content and values.

Leadership = Function (Position, Content, Values)

The next question in my mind was whether all the three variables had an equal impact on leadership. As I studied the transitions further, I found that position and content could explain some parts of the leadership difference. However, the huge swings were really caused by values. Going back to our previous example, Smita was a very strong leader with exceptional followership and influence. Two years after the transition, it was clear to me that Rita did not have even a small fraction of the followership and influence that Smita had. However, as mentioned earlier, Rita was a member of Smita's team and had helped Smita develop much of her content. It was obvious that content and position were not the reasons why Rita's leadership was much less than Smita's. I observed that Rita could not inspire the trust that Smita had; Rita was seen to be principally focused on meeting the needs of her boss and other seniors and, in the process, she had lost the trust of her peers and the rank and file of her team and the organization. It showed me that given a rough similarity in position and content, values were the extraordinary driver of a leader's followership and influence. A 50 per cent difference in content can cause some difference in leadership, but even 10 per cent less in values can create a much bigger swing in leadership. And hence the equation for leadership started to look like this in my mind:

$$\text{Leadership} = (\text{Position} + \text{Content}) \times \text{Values}$$

It was clear to me that position and content were the raw materials for creating leadership impact. If there is no content, even the highest values don't create leadership. Such a person would be liked a lot, but would not have influence and would not be followed. Equally, position does play a role. A very junior person will find it difficult to create followership on a large scale, albeit junior folks with good content do generate significant influence. So position and content go hand-in-hand. But the explosive conversion of that raw material into the finished product of leadership is driven by values, and that is why I saw it as a multiplicative equation for values. For a given position and content, the extent of leadership difference that values can create is staggering.

I then tried to validate this equation through what we see around us on a daily basis, and through some of the great leadership impacts we have seen in India over time. The standout example for me on the impact values can have on leadership is the father of the nation, Mahatma Gandhi. All of us know of the staggering followership he generated, the extraordinary influence he had on the population of the country. If we decode his leadership drivers using my equation, you will find that position was not a big driver for his leadership. He never occupied any important position, he did not come from a powerful political family. He was one of the many leaders who wanted to contribute to the cause of independence. But over time, despite not having the advantage of a formal position, he grew to become the pre-eminent leader of the independence movement. Moving from position, if we examine Gandhiji's content, it was about the independence movement, and many leaders had similar content, though each expressed it in their own ways and words. So it is debatable whether his content was the reason he got such extraordinary followership and influence. Whether superior to others or not, Gandhiji did bring in sound content—his expression of the demand for independence through non-violence and ahimsa was powerful raw material for building leadership impact. But where the explosive impact of leadership kicked in was in the values, the multiplicative factor of my equation. Gandhiji's values are legendary—we have all heard and read about them. Starting with pristine honesty, to being humble enough to clean his own toilet, to the extreme simplicity in what he did, how he lived, the food he ate, his values are folklore. And those exemplary values meant that every single Indian was willing to trust and follow Gandhiji through a most difficult journey of securing independence, which often included severe sacrifices. The leadership equation I developed was validated in my mind—yes, position and content do make a difference, but values make a multiplicative difference to the leadership impact you can have.

Coming to more recent times, many of us in India were witness to the anti-corruption movement that generated a massive followership under the leadership of Anna Hazare in 2011. Let us examine the leadership impact that Anna Hazare had, the followership he commanded and the influence he enjoyed. Again, interestingly, Anna Hazare had no position. He was not the leader of any large party nor was he in the government or in the opposition; he was principally an activist. If we examine the content, we realize that it was anti-corruption. Anti-corruption as content has existed in India for a long time now. Many leaders have espoused the cause, elections have been fought on it. One could argue that it was not original content. Anna did tweak the anti-corruption content to have a face in the Lokpal Bill, so there was something specific for people to grasp, rather than just generic anti-corruption. However, I still believe that content was not the primary reason Anna Hazare generated the followership, influence and impact he had in 2011. The missing puzzle piece was values, which was the extraordinary driver of Anna's leadership impact. With no significant position and oft-used anti-corruption content, but magnified by the multiplicative impact of his values, Anna Hazare achieved a huge followership. Many others with superior position and similar anti-corruption content have seldom managed to create any followership. The staggering difference is in values, the multiplicative driver of leadership.

So overall, I do feel reasonably confident in my equation of leadership. To remind readers again, I measure leadership by the extent of followership and influence. And in that equation, values are the multiplicative factor. I call it the VML equation, short for Values, the Multiplicative driver of Leadership.

$$\text{Leadership} = (\text{Position} + \text{Content}) \times \text{Values}$$

I am sure by now you are saying, yes, I understand that leadership is all about the followership and influence you can create and yes, I understand that values are the multiplicative factor. But does this have anything to do with career success? It does, and at two levels—how leadership helps generate success and what the probability of high values leadership is.

Leadership's Impact on Success

Consider Aditya Puri at HDFC Bank, who transformed the banking industry from a staid, PSU-led industry to a thriving, technology-led customer-centric industry. Consider Anand Kripalu, who transformed Cadbury from a highly recognized and respected small company to a food giant in India. I could go on and quote more examples, but the key is the common theme in these examples—the theme of transformational change.

Great career success always comes on the back of great change and transformation. If you see great careers, you will find that each one of those people drove great transformations and change in their career journeys. I have not seen great careers built on maintaining status quo. To drive transformational change, position gives you the authority and content is what you create for the change that is needed, but it's the followership that you generate that will ensure that people in your team and your organization follow you through that difficult journey of transformational change. And the key to that leadership is the values you bring to the table. Hence, values are a huge driver of career success. People who create the position and content for change journeys, but can't generate the requisite followership and influence, lead failed change journeys. They don't have the values to generate the leadership impact required. To put it simply, great success requires you to drive great change, great change requires you to have great leadership impact and to have great leadership impact you need to have great values. In effect, great success requires the catalyst of great values.

The Probability of High Values

Let's go back to our VML equation,

$$\text{Leadership} = (\text{Position} + \text{Content}) \times \text{Values}$$

We discussed that transformative success is dependent on leadership and hence the probability of having a transformative legacy creating success is equal to the probability of developing very high leadership. In the VML equation, position is something a lot of people eventually get to if they work long enough. Content is again something most people get to, especially with the highly educated population we have. However, exemplary values, the multiplicative factor of the VML equation, is a tough nut to crack. Exemplary values are easy to read about, but difficult to develop and practise consistently, and hence there is a lower probability to achieve the level of leadership that transformative success requires. That is why many people get leadership positions and content, but very few can leverage them into legacy-creating transformational change. The probability of developing high values is low, and hence, if you want to be a legacy-creating leader, start fighting the values battle straightaway. It is a battle very few fight and even fewer win.

Now, you are probably saying, yes, I understand the VML equation and yes, I will embrace values as a driver of success, but which values are we talking about? I will not give you a scientifically validated answer for that—it is too complex a question for me to answer. However, I will share my thinking on this subject. There are many values—honesty/integrity, simplicity, humility, authenticity . . . the list could go on. My belief is that you must maintain a high level overall in all values and you must be an exemplar in a few, your 'lodestar values', where you are head and shoulders above anyone else. I think that is the combination that creates leadership impact. That is the approach I have taken, and I want to share with you my journey and experience in trying to develop my lodestar values. I embraced the twin Hs— honesty and humility—as my lodestar values. I will share my experience and understanding of these two values in the coming chapter, and I do hope it inspires you to create your own journey of pursuing your own lodestar values.

12

The Twin Hs: The Key Catalysts for Leadership Impact

The first value I want to talk about is honesty, often also referred to as integrity. I like the simpler and broader term honesty, so let us use that for this chapter. I have no doubt in my mind that pristine honesty is an extraordinary driver of leadership impact. It is the one value which, if embraced in its truest form, will give you immense, loyal followership and influence. The challenge with honesty is, how does one set the standard for honesty, pristine honesty at that? In my fifty years, I have met possibly hundreds of thousands of people. I am yet to meet even one person who believes that they are dishonest. Each one of us believes that we are honest. The reason for that is that there is no set standard for it. There is no specification or control standard that says this is the level above which you are an honest person and below which you are dishonest. Hence, each one of us feels we are honest, not because of our absolute level of honesty, but because we always set the standard lower than our current personal honesty level.

If you want to set a high benchmark for values, with honesty as your core lodestar value, then the starting point has to be defining a standard of honesty for yourself. Let me try and do that for you with the help of the diagram below.

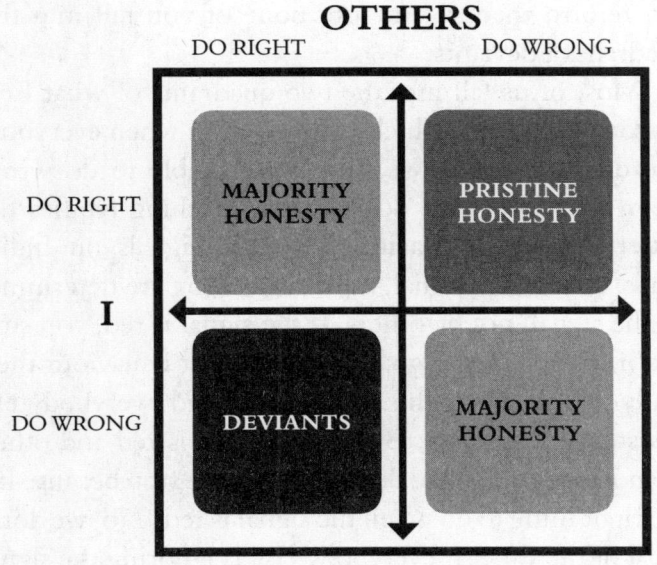

As you can see in that diagram, on the Y axis is 'I' and there are two boxes—'I do right' and 'I do wrong'. On the X axis is 'others', and there are two boxes—'others do right' and 'others do wrong'.

We will use this diagram to understand our current standard of honesty and then try and see how we can set a new standard for ourselves.

The quadrant of 'I do wrong', even when 'others do right', is what I like to call the quadrant of 'deviants'. This is the small minority of the population who does wrong even when everybody else is doing right. They are the criminals, the frauds, the harassers, the embezzlers, etc. They are a small minority. I hope God will bless them and reform them. I am sure none of you fall into that quadrant of deviants.

Most of us fall into the two quadrants of what I call 'majority honesty', which is we do right when everybody else does right, but we find it acceptable to do wrong when everybody else does wrong. Nothing typifies this better than our behaviour at traffic signals on Indian roads. At a traffic signal, right and wrong are determined by the signal, not by others. If the signal is red, you stop, and if it's green, you go. But what is our behaviour there really driven by? If the signal is red and everybody else has stopped, we stop. But if the signal is red and others are not stopping, what do we do? Do we stop because it is the right thing to do when the signal is red? No, we don't, most of the time. If everybody else is ignoring the signal, we ignore it too. In effect, we find it easy to do wrong because everybody else is also doing wrong. And when we do wrong that way, we don't think we are dishonest; we think it is acceptable for honest people to do wrong because everybody else is doing wrong as well. That does not make us dishonest in our own eyes.

Even our Indian biological constitution is that way. When I am on the streets of Mumbai and I feel spit rising to my mouth, then my biological constitution is such that I cannot keep that spit in my mouth—it must come out on to the streets of Mumbai. And then one day, I take a five-hour flight to Singapore. I land in the pristine, clean city, and suddenly, my body changes. The spit in my mouth refuses to come out on to the streets of Singapore. Despite years of spitting in Mumbai, just one five-hour flight can change how my spit behaves.

Apologies for the sarcasm in the para above, but as you can see, I want to drive home the concept of majority honesty. We find it acceptable to spit on Mumbai streets because everybody else is doing it. But the moment we land in Singapore, where others are not spitting, we suddenly feel it's wrong to spit on the streets. And then after a week, another five-hour return flight to Mumbai and majority honesty kicks in. Suddenly, spitting on the street is acceptable again. Spitting, in the above anecdote, is simply an example to explain the concept. It applies to all those things like not standing in a line, giving or taking bribes, leaving toilets dirty, etc., which we do just because everybody else does them too.

The basic construct of majority honesty is that what we use as the standard of honesty, the standard to determine what is right and wrong, is not our own judgement, our own moral compass. Instead, it is based on what the majority does, and if the majority gets away with doing something wrong, then doing wrong becomes honesty for us too.

Hence, if we want to be truly honest, to be considered someone with high integrity, to be among the small percentage of population that can truly stand up and say 'I am genuinely honest', then we have to change our standard of honesty. If you truly want to be honest, then you must have the courage to do right even when everybody else does wrong. You must move to the quadrant of pristine honesty. The quadrant of pristine honesty is when I do right, even when others do wrong.

The crucial change required to move to the pristine honesty quadrant is changing the reference standard of what is honest—from 'what the majority does' to 'what I think is right'. It is an easy change to describe in words, a difficult one to execute in life. Let me give you a simple example from my own life. When I joined a new company, there was an existing culture of all meetings starting late and ending late. In the early days, I also fell into that trap of being late to meetings. Basically, I was doing what others did—I had allowed my standard to change from what is right to what others were doing. Then one fine day, the realization dawned. I realized that despite all my preaching on honesty, I was not practising it on the simplest of things like being on time for meetings, even if others were not. Then I reoriented myself to saying I will do what I think is right, which is to be on time for meetings, even if others are late. It is a simple example to demonstrate that pristine honesty is a difficult thing to practise. Every now and then, there is a temptation to lapse into 'since others do wrong, it is acceptable for me also to do wrong'. You have to constantly remind yourself and focus on doing what you think is right and take a decision that you will not do anything wrong simply because everyone else does it.

The impact of pristine honesty as a catalyst on greater leadership impact is extraordinary. Truly great leaders have often been inflexibly obdurate on what they believe is right, even against tremendous popular sentiment. Going back to Gandhiji, the number of times he stood firm in his beliefs, even when the entire population stood against him, is well-documented. There were times he went on a fast to death because he believed the entire population was doing something wrong and he was willing to stake his life on what he thought was right, even if it was against popular sentiment.

The story is the same in the corporate world. Truly great leaders have stood for what they believe is right, even against popular sentiment in their companies. This pristine honesty and integrity, over time, is what has given them the leadership impact, the extraordinary followership and influence, which very few corporate leaders are ever able to build. Most corporate leaders are not able to successfully build leadership impact based on their values beyond the leadership impact created by their position. You have that choice—do you want to be among the many leaders who are primarily governed by popular opinion or do you want to be among the few leaders who are governed by what they believe is right? If you want to be among the very few leaders who are larger than life, who are beyond the chair and the position they occupy, and who are legacy-creating, then you have to catalyse your leadership with the power of pristine honesty.

The Other H, Humility

The second value I want to talk about is the other H, humility. I want to describe this value from my own context to start with. I believe I am reasonably successful in my work life. I have operated at several senior positions and created impact. When you get to senior levels in the corporate world, you do kind of get a demi-god status, and people in the company might often flatter you. It is possible to allow this to go to your head and for you to start thinking that you are indeed extraordinary. I have always desperately tried to remind myself that I am just another person. I just happen to be successful in my career and that does not make me God. I try not to fly too high and always keep my feet on the ground. And talking of feet, I want to tell you the story about my feet and legs.

I was born with a severe deformity. All of us have our knees in front of our legs. When I was born, the knee on my left leg was on the back side of my leg. My family used to say that it was because I bent my left leg at the knee such that my feet moved in the direction of my chest when I was born. It was but obvious that with that kind of deformity, I would possibly never be able to walk in my life.

Now, this was in the late 1960s in Chennai. Within a very short time, my family took me to most orthopaedics in the city. None of the doctors had seen many cases like mine and there was no clear solution in sight. My family was of limited means, and they could not afford to fly me to a different city or country to assess the situation and seek treatment.

I had an extraordinary grandmother, a lady who never went to school, got married at fourteen and had five kids by the age of twenty-two, with my mother being her eldest. I have no doubt that if she were born in the modern era, with more equal opportunities for both genders, she would have at the very least headed a country—truly a courageous lady with great capacity for decision-making and consensus-building. She, along with my parents, was faced with the decision on what to do with me in this situation, where no doctor was willing to assure complete success of the treatment. They had to make two decisions—one, whether they should take the risk of a very complex treatment on a newborn for which there was no guarantee of success and, two, which doctor to go to, since none of the doctors promised success. Everybody gave them probabilities.

They took both decisions. They took the first decision of going ahead with the treatment. The logic was simple, they said, let us give the boy a chance. In the worst case scenario, a failed treatment, the risk to life was minimal, and so it simply meant that I lived with the deformity my whole life, which would have been the case anyway if they did not do anything. In hindsight, an easy, obvious decision, but it took tremendous courage and foresight from my family to make it under those difficult, stressful circumstances. The second decision was which doctor to go to—again, not an easy decision to make. Each had their own approach to that situation and again, my family made the right choice (I shall not reveal the name of the doctor for privacy reasons, but I remain ever grateful to that person for my life).

The doctor did a great job. My family tells me I was flat on the bed for more than a year. I did not start walking, like most kids, before the age of two; there are many versions to when I started walking, but most of them agree that I took my first step not before the age of three. My earliest memories are of having a very large metallic contraption on my left leg, from my hip to my foot, with which I would go to school in the beginning. But life moved on and I could soon walk normally.

In my thirties, I started tasting success in my work life. One day, my grandmother sat me down. She said, I am so proud of you for being successful, but never forget why you are here. You are here because Dr X had the skill to successfully carry out a difficult treatment many decades ago. He could do it in an era when neither the technology nor the resources for such a complex procedure was available. His skill and the prayers of the family are why you are here, why you are what you are. I still remember that day, and the way she said it hit me. I was facing the first flush of success in my career, starting to fly a bit, starting to think I am Superman. That day, I landed on my feet, on those feet which were deformed when I was born and then corrected, thanks to the decisions my family took and to the skill of the doctor. Ever since then, I have stayed on my feet, no matter how successful I have been.

When I was in my early forties, I ran my first half-marathon. I covered 21 km in 2 hours and 52 minutes. Not great by any athletic standards, but given how I was born, possibly a small miracle that I could run at all. After I had crossed the finish line, I called my grandmother and told her what I had managed to do, and she cried on the phone that day. And true to her style, again told me, never forget why you are able to run, never forget why you are able to lead the life you are living.

It's indeed the truth—my success in life can be attributed to the decisions my family took and to the skill of the doctor. If my family had got its decisions wrong or if the doctor had got something wrong, I would probably never have walked. It might have meant I never went to school, never got educated, never worked, never became successful in my career and never wrote this book either. Yet, when I was successful, it would have been easy for me to forget this and start to think the reason for my success was what I had done, to lose my humility and to think I and I alone made it happen.

In the corporate world, quite often, one does come across people who change a lot with success, who lose touch with humility, with themselves, and start to function a few feet off the ground in their minds.

One of my favourite quotes is, 'You are not as good as your best success; you are not as bad as your worst failure.' We are clearly in a highly VUCA-filled world, where success and failure both happen at a fair pace. The best of companies and the best of leaders experience them. Failure, especially, seems to rear its head when there is much success, when you start to think nothing can go wrong, when you lose touch with humility.

Humility is the value that I believe grounds people. It is this value that allows you to be centred and not fly off when you experience success. If you are humble, you know that no success is ever created by you alone; there are other people involved, there are circumstances that contributed to your success, and so on. Humility allows you to enjoy the success without letting it affect you, without it creating arrogance in you. Equally, the grounded nature of a humble person is what also allows him or her to deal with failure when it happens. If you are humble, your ability to stay grounded through cycles of success and failure is much higher, and your ability to sustain long-term success is much higher as well.

Humility has a tremendous impact on leadership and in creating followership. Often, powerful leaders are those who have a very ambitious vision, but have the humility to not let that ambitious vision make them arrogant. Such people create a sense of 'cause' in their teams and organizations because their humility is what assures people that the leader is chasing the ambition not for his or her personal gain, but because it is the right thing to do, because they believe in it. When there is a powerful vision and a leader who, because of their humility, is seen to be chasing that vision for unselfish reasons, then that combination is effective in creating leadership impact.

13

Values, the Catalyst for Leadership Impact

Let's again come back to the why of values. Yes, there is a moral dimension to it, but that is not the sole reason why I believe it is important. I believe it is a catalyst that helps you succeed. As I said earlier,

$$\text{Leadership} = (\text{Position} + \text{Content}) \times \text{Values}$$

I seek to change your understanding of values from a coding that says limit the downside of poor values to a coding that says leverage the upside of superior values. And that upside is the multiplicative impact that values have on the leadership impact you can have. I described the values that I have been particularly passionate about, the twin Hs of honesty and humility. I have no doubt that my values created the multiplicative impact in my leadership. I am passionate about each one of you using values as a catalyst for creating leadership impact. So create

174

your own values journey—it has a tremendous impact on your long-term success and, of course, it has the moral advantage of making you a better person too.

Once you decide that you want to use values as a catalyst in creating leadership impact and success, the question is, how do you develop these lodestar values? I find that most people believe in the myth that values are intrinsic and that they do not need to be worked upon. If we need to improve our technical skills, we work on them. If we have to improve our physical fitness, we work on it. But when it comes to values, we don't consciously try to improve them, we never have a values improvement programme for ourselves. We think that just leading our lives every day is enough to improve our values. I do think that is a myth. While there is something intrinsic about values, they also need work to improve. Much like how simply spending time at work does not build experience, much like how just going up the corporate ladder does not automatically improve productivity, living life every day does not improve values. Improvement in values has to be catalysed, especially if you want it to reach the level of being a lodestar value.

My own journey of improving my values has been a highly rewarding one, not to mention challenging. I would say that till about my late thirties, I was firmly in the camp of majority honesty myself, feeling no qualms about doing wrong when others did wrong. And then once I decided I wanted to change my standard of honesty to pristine honesty, of doing what I thought was right, even if others were doing wrong and getting away with it, it was not easy. It was like any other skill improvement programme; it needed working on.

The simplest thing I started with was to set myself goals in areas where I would not do wrong just because others did wrong. E.g. I set myself the goal that I would never do wrong at a traffic signal even if everybody else was not following the signal. I also set myself the goal that if I use a public toilet, I will always leave it clean for the next person, irrespective of how dirty I found it, irrespective of the fact that several people do not bother to leave public toilets clean after they use them. These are areas where it is very easy to follow majority honesty principles and do wrong, and I said to myself, I will start by changing in these areas. While it might look like a few trivial things, the way it worked for me was each time one of these instances happened, when I stood at a traffic signal when everybody was breaking it or when I made the effort to leave a public toilet clean, it was reinforcing in my own mind the concept of pristine honesty.

I did this for a year or so, after which the next step I took was to build it into my daily reflection in the evening on my way back in the car. Every evening, along with the question 'What could I have done better?' I would reflect on whether there were any instances where I practised majority honesty that day. That reflection would make me realize some uncomfortable things. E.g. in the workplace, one of the most practised forms of majority honesty is when the boss does something wrong and nobody confronts him or her with it. People know the boss has done wrong, people know the right thing in the interest of the company is to point it out, yet the majority honesty approach is that when nobody else is doing it, why should I stick my neck out and point it out? I struggled with this one. My pristine honesty always told me, Mouli, every time you find something wrong being done by people senior to you, you need to have the courage to point it out with good intent for improvement, not fault-finding. I did it more often than most people. Yet, sometimes, it was difficult to implement, and I would lapse to majority honesty. I am just giving this as an example to demonstrate how improvement in values is not easy to accomplish. It is quite complex and it needs working at it in a sustained way.

My learning is that there are three stages to values improvement:

1. The first stage is sensitivity—facing what you are doing well in that value and what you are doing poorly. Creating self-awareness of how you fare at the lodestar standard of that value is the very starting point of improving it.

2. The second stage is practice—forcing yourself to practise the right values behaviour. Choosing a few clear practice areas and being extremely disciplined in practising these will help build the consciousness of the lodestar standard in you.

3. The third stage is embedding it into the person you are—the stage where the practice no longer requires conscious effort but gets integrated into who you are.

Values are among the most difficult things to be good at, and to be at a lodestar level is challenging, to say the least. It is easier to be a smart chemical engineer than to practise pristine honesty. It is easier to be a marketing genius than it is to be truly humble. Values improvement to a lodestar level has to be catalysed by you through an improvement plan. It will not happen by itself.

Unleash the Catalyst

1. The bulk of the corporate culture on values is to restrict the occurrence of a breach. I, however, believe there is an upside to superior values for long-term success. For that, it is essential to change the coding of your understanding on values, from one that says limit the downside to one that says leverage the upside.
2. The upside of catalysing values comes from the higher leadership impact that superior values can create. Leadership impact is measured by the followership and influence that you have. Leadership impact as per the VML equation is driven by position and content and, most importantly, values, which have a multiplicative impact on leadership.
3. The values I believed in were the twin Hs, honesty and humility. The key to honesty is to reach the level of pristine honesty, which means you focus on doing right even when others are doing wrong and getting away with it. Humility is about staying grounded through cycles of success and failure, knowing that you alone are not the reason for your success.

4. Leadership impact based on superior values allows you to drive transformational change based on strong followership. It is transformational change that is the sign of a legacy-creating leader, and allows you to create long-term success for yourself.

5. Superior values have to be catalysed through an improvement plan. Just living your life every day does not improve your values; you have to work towards improving them.

6. Remember, great success requires you to drive great change, great change requires you to have great leadership impact and to have great leadership impact, you need to have great values. In effect, great success requires the catalyst of great values.

14

Bringing It All Together

We began by discussing that career success is a function of real individual growth. Hence, if you focus on driving real individual growth, career success will follow as a consequence.

In Part I, we spoke about catalysing the experience algorithm using the TMRR process and leveraging learning cycles. We also spoke of the need to grow your personal productivity as you climb up the corporate ladder. I think of experience algorithm and personal productivity as the necessary raw materials for success. These are the foundational blocks. Without the raw material of the experience algorithm and productivity, it is difficult to create career success even if you have good values. In my judgement, a large majority, say between 70–80 per cent of people, can catalyse the development of the necessary raw materials to have meaningful success in their careers. And if you truly embrace the catalysts of TMRR, learning cycles and productivity drivers, then you will build an algorithm that is going to set you up for exceptional success, not moderate success.

However, the raw materials alone are not enough. The catalyst of good career decisions is required to convert it into career success as covered in Part II. The key principle is to take decisions that catalyse real individual growth in the first half, which will help you succeed when it matters, in the second half of your career. Having good bosses in the foundational stage of your career and having mentors who help you with decision-making in a VUCA career world are crucial catalysts for good career choices. The most important career decisions to make are the decisions to quit and join, and segregating the two, making them independently and based on learning and fit, will get you to make the right choices.

In my judgement here, over 50 per cent of people do not manage their careers well. The biggest mistake is managing the first half for success in the first half only, as opposed to foundation-building for the second half. The other key mistake is poor quit and join decisions based on trappings rather than intrinsic factors. Hence, of the 70–80 per cent who manage to develop the necessary raw materials of the algorithm and the productivity, over 50 per cent do not achieve the success they deserve due to career mistakes. Combining the right raw materials and the right career decisions, as an aggregate, we are down to 35–40 per cent whose success in their careers is commensurate with their potential.

In Part III, we spoke of how we can bring the 'life' of 'work–life' into work, how the way you live your life can be a catalyst for your success at work. Developing a 'passionate striving' hobby is the catalyst that allows you to meet your achievement need outside work and thus helps you operate from mastery and purpose at work. That, coupled with the leadership impact that superior values can create, can place you in the highest echelons of success. If you truly want to break free of the 35–40 per cent mentioned earlier and if your aspiration is for legacy-creating leadership and the breakout success that very few achieve, then you have to bring the catalyst of life into work. You have to bring the power of who you are, your values, your passion, into work, and you have to keep improving these. Very few people bring the power of their entire being to success at work. Very few develop the level of values required to become legacy-creating leaders who leave an impact. If that is your aspiration then you have to set a standard for yourself to be in the 1–2 per cent of the highest values-driven, self-aware individuals. A challenging task, but not impossible.

The other key aspect I want to deal with is how you use this book and its learning. Do not think of it as sequential sections—I have to build the algorithm first, then I have to make good career choices and then I will think about life and values and hobbies. It is not sequential. At the time you are reading this book, you already have an algorithm. While you must make the effort to develop it further, you must also make good career choices for the algorithm you already have. Hence, you must make good Part II career choices even as you start the Part I journey of TMRR to further improve your algorithm. And as for integrating life and values, it is never too early to start that journey. The junior-most people, even students, can embark on that journey of improving who they are. So my sincere advice is to embrace all the three sections of the book and not see them as sequential.

My other recommendation for benefiting from this book is to read it more than once. Reading it a few times will get the whole structure in your head and build more conviction. I would also recommend that once a month, you pick up any one chapter and read it. It will be a refresher and make a tremendous difference in your quest for success.

My vision for you—my wish for each one of you who reads this book—is that this book becomes the catalyst that inspires you to be among the 1–2 per cent of people with the highest success. All the best. May the force be with you.

The Final Question

I do hope each one of you achieves the success that you want in your career by dint of your efforts, and with this book as a catalyst. However, it does bring us to the final question—why do you want to succeed in your career? Is success a means to an end or is it an end in itself? 'Why do I want to succeed?' is an important question you must ask yourself.

My own journey in this regard has seen change over time. When I started working, in the early days, success was all about knowing that I was good enough. It was about material progress and career achievement. Over time, it evolved to a degree of personal pride, not the arrogant kind, but a degree of pride in being successful. But as is obvious, none of these were meaningful enough and hence, none of them stuck for long. Then, after fifteen years of working, I got an opportunity to be in the HR function for a few years. In those few years, unknown to myself, I started to develop a sense of mission. It was about making a difference to people around me, making them better, making them productive and making them more successful. And, over time, I became more and more conscious of it, and started to realize that when I do things with the mission of impacting people around me positively, I get a tremendous sense of focus and energy. And when I did stuff with that energy and mission, I started doing even better, getting more effective and productive.

Slowly, I started building that as a personal mission—the mission of making people I reach out to better because of their interactions with me. I wanted to help them realize their dreams, understand themselves better and become their best selves. This did not mean I did not focus on work and results at work, but this was why I was chasing results at work. It meant small changes. It meant that when I set a high ambition, part of my mission was to produce results, but part of it was also to coach and develop people in that process. It meant that when I travelled to various offices of my company, I always took the time out to interact with the people in that office on a very meaningful basis, not just for me to know what they were doing but also to try and make a small difference in their effectiveness and life. It meant that when I read a book, not only did I use it for my own improvement but I also spoke about it to others to help them make a small difference.

The 'Tee off with Mouli' sessions, which I mentioned in the beginning, were a direct result of this mission. And writing this book, taking off from the sessions, is part of the same mission of helping make people better. That does not mean I do not have the same ambition for the success of this book as any other author has for the success of his or her book. I have the same ambition, I want this book to succeed, but my success has a purpose—it is a means to an end, not an end in itself. My success has the purpose of making everybody who reads this book better at work, better in their learning, better in how they live their lives and better people who will further propagate the good messages in this book to try to make a difference to people around them. And that sense of purpose gives me even more fuel to try and succeed with this book than if I had written this book without a sense of mission.

Hence, here is my final question to you at the end of this book. I know you want to succeed, otherwise you might not have reached the end of the book. But do you know why you want to succeed? What is success the means to in your life?

This book will help you in the journey of success, but finding the purpose behind why you want to succeed is something that you must do for yourself.

Acknowledgements

I have to start by acknowledging those who helped me in my journey in the corporate world. If it had not been for this journey, I would never have built the learning and insights required to write a book like this. Foremost in this have been the two influential bosses of mine, Anand Kripalu and Bharat Puri. I am also deeply thankful to a set of leaders and colleagues who have inspired and taught me: P.M. Murty, Ashwinbhai Dani, Ashwinbhai Choksi, Abhaybhai Vakil, Jalaj Dani, Manish Choksi, K.B.S. Anand, Amit Syngle and P.G. Ponnapa from Asian Paints; Gulu Mirchandani, Vijay Mansukhani, G. Sundar and Sasha Mirchandani from Onida; and Todd Stitzer, Ken Hannah, Marck Reckitt, Bob Stack, Rajiv Wahi, Nick Fell, Amit Banati, Irene Rosenfeld, Tim Cofer, Karen May, Mary Beth West, Manu Anand and Pradeep Pant from Cadbury/Mondelez. I am also thankful to the partners I have worked with who have been great teachers and friends: Piyush Pandey, Madhukar Sabnavis, Govind

Pandey, Kinu, Hepsibah Pathak, Sonali and Ganapathy from Ogilvy; Ravi Deshpande, Umesh Shrikhande and Rohit Shrivastav from Contract and Lemon and thereafter; Sam Balsara, Bikram Sakhuja, Dnyanadha, Shekhar and Gautam from Madison; and Vispy Doctor, Jasmeet, Gita and Meera from my research agencies. Each one of them has contributed in some way to what I have learnt and some of their teachings are what is reflected in this book.

I also want to thank those who made the writing of this book possible. I must start with those who triggered the thought that I must write a book. While many people have often told me that I must write one, had it not been for the prodding of Govind Pandey, Savitha Shivshankar and Chavvi Bindal, I might not have even seriously considered this. I must thank my publishers Penguin Random House for readily accepting my synopsis and being tremendous partners in this journey. I want to thank all the teams in Penguin Random House for making this happen—your commitment and professionalism are outstanding. A special thanks to my editor Radhika Marwah for her partnership with me.

I want to thank my author friends Ambi Parameswaran and Prakash Iyer for providing a debutant author like me some valuable tips. I am also indebted to my current employers, Pidilite Industries, M.B. Parekh and Bharat Puri for giving me the space and encouragement to write a book. I am thankful to Anand Kriplau, Siddartha Mukherjee and my brothers Balaji and Swami for reviewing the book and giving me valuable feedback. Many thanks to Harish Thawani and the staff of Indus

Club, where I have sat many a day from morning till evening writing the book, for providing a fantastic environment. I also want to thank a core group of dear friends who have selflessly helped me in the marketing of this book. God bless them.

Lastly I want to thank every company where I did 'Tee off with Mouli' sessions, the leaders who invited me there and every participant of these sessions. The energy I got from them was phenomenal and the questions they asked helped me sharpen every point I have made in this book. Thank you all.

Scan QR code to access the
Penguin Random House India website